Walks in Mysterious North Lakeland

Graham Dugdale

SIGMA
Leisure

Published by Sigma Leisure – an imprint of
Sigma Press, 1 South Oak Lane, Wilmslow, Cheshire SK9 6AR, England.

British Library Cataloguing in Publication Data
A CIP record for this book is available from the British Library.

ISBN: 1-85058-626-8

Typesetting and Design by: Sigma Press, Wilmslow, Cheshire.

Cover photograph: Castlerigg Stone Circle with Blencathra standing guard (Graham Dugdale)

Maps and photographs: Graham Dugdale

Printed by: MFP Design and Print

Disclaimer: the information in this book is given in good faith and is believed to be correct at the time of publication. No responsibility is accepted by either the author or publisher for errors or omissions, or for any loss or injury howsoever caused. Only you can judge your own fitness, competence and experience.

Foreword

In old times, travelling in the wilds of Cumberland might be beset with fears of the dreadful unknown. Unless you carried a sprig of rowan, you might be unlucky enough to meet Old Nick, or some hideous bogle, or see the black dog, the carrier of ill news.

In the 18th century, when the Lakes were getting their first tourists, some still believed that mountains were wastelands and barriers, objects of horror. Just to be amongst them excited the imagination. The natives, eager to enjoy the new wealth that tourism was bringing, could hardly be blamed for encouraging the enthusiasm and excitement by spinning a yarn or two. The old stories, imaginative or factual, told by the winter firesides, were resurrected and elaborated. There is hardly a valley in the Lake District which does not have its tale.

Of course, we don't believe the ghost stories any more, do we? Well, there are quite a few places into which your modern, sophisticated Cumbrian will not venture on dark nights.

There are two things in life which are amongst the most pleasing: a good country walk and a good story. Graham Dugdale describes walks in atmospheric Northern Lakeland, and spices them with a tale or two. What more could you ask?

John Wyatt - *Retired Chief Ranger of the Lake District*

Prologue

O'er all there hung a shadow and a fear;
A sense of mystery the spirit daunted,
And said as plain as whisper in the ear,
The place is haunted.

Thomas Hood, The Haunted House

Once more, readers are invited to journey back into the singularly inscrutable world of our region's hazy past. To travel boldly, probing deep into mysteries long forgotten. On this occasion our goal is to investigate the broad spectrum of legendary happenings in and around North Lakeland.

But who shall determine where truth fades into obscurity, to be replaced by mystical folklore handed down through generations by word of mouth? Certainly not I. Where myth and legend are concerned, interpretation remains a matter for individual cognisance.

We are fortunate that these storytellers possessed a ready wit and a flair for the dramatic that have assisted in creating an amalgam of titillating yarns that only Cumbrians could have devised. Sitting round a roaring fire with the wind howling down the chimney, no listener could fail to be stirred by the colourful renditions.

These thirty walks visit all manner of bizarre and enigmatic locales and complement those in the companion volume for South Lakeland. Together, they form a comprehensive assemblage of fascinating events relevant to our Cumbrian heritage.

Some of the stories are well documented, with hard evidence in support of their claim to immortality. Such is the case of Thomas Bland who created his unique Garden of Images at Reagill. Or, indeed, Mary Robinson, the so-called Beauty of Buttermere, who lived at the Fish Inn and who was buried in the churchyard at Caldbeck.

Others are clearly the result of fervid speculation and an over-indulgent mind, often concocted by simple folk to explain a world of which they had little understanding. That was doubtless the situation which led to the highest point of the Pennines being named Fiend's Fell. The Devil had much to answer for in primordial Lakeland. Especially at Stenkrith Bridge near Kirkby Stephen where his 'Mustard Mill' generated a hot sweat amongst locals.

But what of the Bishop of Barf? And who can furnish the original meaning of Dacre's Four Bears? Some mysteries merely serve to encourage an active stimulation of the grey matter. And that can be no bad thing either. For as the eminent scholar Albert Einstein once observed, 'Imagination is more important than knowledge.'

Laugh at Jack Wilson's claim to have witnessed the last fairies in Westmorland by all means. Pour scorn upon the waters of Bowscale Tarn's immortal trout if you must. But whatever your views regarding the validity or otherwise of the mysteries under investigation, no fell rambler worthy of the name can deny the rich scenic value of the walks on offer.

Mind-boggling, sinister, outlandish and eccentric, all of them are nothing short of intriguing. They will open up previously neglected areas of Lakeland - so expect some odd glances from people unused to eyeballing strangers in their midst. Approach haunted places with a sense of unease; feel the chilled ripple of fear trickling down your spine; experience a chattering of teeth and a trembling of bones in the presence of denizens from below. But most of all, enjoy the walks as much as I did and you will have truly experienced Lakeland at its very best.

Acknowledgements

Many thanks to Philip Cavener of NeeBee Boots for his continued support and Don Cooper of Lowe Alpine in Kendal.

Graham Dugdale

Contents

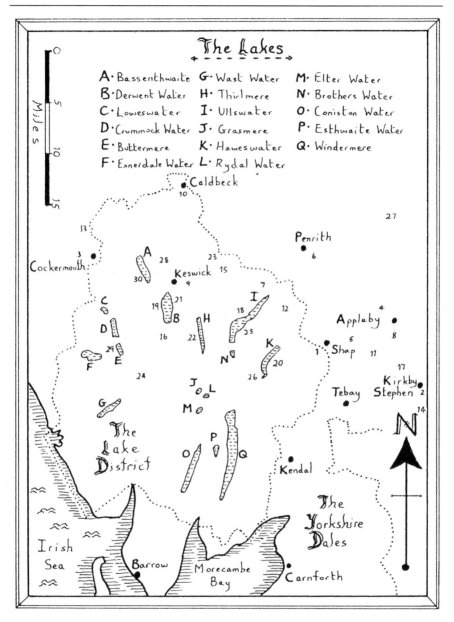

The Lakes

A · Bassenthwaite   G · Wast Water   M · Elter Water
B · Derwent Water   H · Thirlmere   N · Brothers Water
C · Loweswater   I · Ullswater   O · Coniston Water
D · Crummock Water   J · Grasmere   P · Esthwaite Water
E · Buttermere   K · Haweswater   Q · Windermere
F · Ennerdale Water L · Rydal Water

Key to Maps

～ A6	Main Roads	⋰⋱	Limestone Pavements
B 5270	Secondary Roads	▲	Summits & Cairns
⤙	Minor Roads	310	Spot Heights
∿⟶	Railways	⋯⋰	Main Walls
⌁	Main rights-of-way	⥲	Main Fences
⤳	Route to follow	⌇	Hedging
≋	Rivers & Streams	P	Parking for Cars
⬭	Lakes & Tarns	⊤	Buildings
⋯	Marshy Ground	⟊	Bridges
⋀⋀⋀	Coniferous Woods	+	Churches
⥾⥾⥾	Deciduous Woods	G	Gates
⥿⥿⥿	Mixed Woodland	S	Stiles
⣿⣿	Steep Crags	FB	Footbridges

About The Walks

The walks in this book are arranged so that the easiest come first and those requiring more effort come later, roughly related to *distance* covered and *height* ascended plus an ingredient labelled *Author's Privilege*. This makes no concession to personal preference, which would most certainly be open to dispute in any case.

Only seven of them visit mountain summits which exceed the magical height of 2000 feet. It is clear, therefore, that the majority of mysterious happenings have taken place at lower altitudes. Ghosts it has to be said, are gregarious entities that rarely venture onto the lonely fell tops. And the myths and legends surrounding bizarre events are primarily associated with the peripheral localities where the storytellers dwelt.

In consequence, they are eminently suitable for all the family to enjoy whilst learning more about the origins of our Lakeland heritage. Armchair explorers with a nose for a good story, and those who simply relish the opportunity to delve beneath the surface in pursuit of an elusive reality are well catered for.

Paths and Maps

Once the public highways are left behind, rights of way are made use of at all times. The maps are meant to ensure that all the walks are self-contained. But no map, however well drawn, can replace the relevant Ordnance Survey sheet, which embodies all the finer details needed to flesh out the walks. Only the most relevant field boundaries have been included, to avoid confusion as well as clutter on the maps. Fencing and hedging often occur together so the dominant feature on each arm of a field has been used.

Walk 1

Shap: Down by the Riverside

Mysteries:	Shap Abbey GR 548152, Goggleby Stone and others GR 159151
Distance:	4 miles
Total Height Climbed:	130 feet (40 metres)
Nearest Centre:	Shap
Start and Finish:	After turning down the Bampton Road at the northern limit of Shap village, take the second left, signposted to Shap Abbey. Leave your car on the English Heritage parking area in the valley bottom.
Map:	Ordnance Survey English Lakes, 1:25 000, north-east area

A brief scan of the Ordnance Survey map for the vicinity of Shap village will reveal an array of primeval artefacts, proving that in this area at least, there was, indeed, life before Chris Evans.

Individualistic, with its own unique character, Shap is what could be termed a 'fence-sitter'. Neither truly Lakeland nor exclusively Pennine in character, its austere location on the bleak, windswept moorland has for aeons given shelter to travellers journeying between Scotland and the South. Not all of these, however, were appreciative of the hospitality offered.

Bonnie Prince Charlie himself, during his march south in 1745, was heard to complain about the quality and cost of his lodgings. And not one hundred years since, the celebrated novelist Anthony Trollope was moved to 'thank Heaven that they had not been born Shappites'; a reference to the inclement weather and bumpy discomfiture experienced on the long coach ride from Kendal.

Fastest of these were the brown and scarlet mail coaches which plied between Preston and Carlisle, passing over Shap Fell, where blockages were frequent. One of the worst winters on record was in 1836, when snow was said to be 'mountain high', reaching beyond the roof of the coach in places. But whatever the conditions, the mail still had to get through. Stranded coaches were abandoned by the guard, who would continue on foot along with his precious cargo of letters.

A first glimpse of Shap Abbey, almost hidden from view alongside the River Lowther, suggests a forlorn, even sad appearance. Reduced to a mere shell by scavenging stone merchants, the lone tower probes the grey mantle overhead, giving barely a hint of its proud lineage. Where once the bustle of industrious endeavour (both spiritual and temporal) controlled the well-being of the local populace, all is now silent.

Yet when you enter the confines of the site and gaze up through the open vault of the tower, a sense of purpose and dominion filters down through centuries. The influence of the monks who laboured and prayed in this austere place was, indeed, considerable. Fleeces from sheep reared on the granges were much sought after by cloth merchants, even in distant Italy.

But life must have been grim to say the least for the Premonstratensian order that lived and worked in these bleak surroundings for over 300 years, until the abbey's dissolution by Henry VIII in 1540. Known as White Canons on account of their distinctive woollen habits, the order took its name from the 12th-century mother abbey founded in the French town of Premontre. Unlike the Franciscans, they were a settled order of monks, preferring to dirty their hands in godly toil.

An equally laudable duty assiduously performed was to provide a travellers' rest along the once busy thoroughfare that followed the Lowther Valley. It would appear that, contrary to later reports, their hospitality was

Stepping stones across the River Lowther

highly regarded, dissolution coming much later to Shap than for many similar establishments.

It is very probable that some guests would have been politely requested to assist with flood relief at those times of the year when the Lowther over-flowed its banks. Warbling in harmony with the Gregorian chanters, the river at least provided a purpose-built sewage disposal facility. But more than just a fervid imagination is needed these days to conjure up the vibrant community of centuries past.

The Walk

Leave the English Heritage site to resume its cloistered musing and climb the steep, grass bank on the east side of the valley. Bear right through a stile to follow the upper, fenced edge of Abbey Wood to its far end, where another stile is crossed.

Stick with the grey, stone wall on the left, passing a small clump of thorn trees. A further 50 metres will bring you to a splendidly stepped crossing point. On the far side of the wall, continue south-east, passing to the right of a wall corner ahead. As the village of Keld is approached, cross a fence stile and the lawn of a private dwelling to reach the main street over a cattle grid.

In company with many other small settlements investigated in this volume, Keld has escaped the tainted hand of commercial exploitation. Few people are likely to make a detour from Shap to visit this old Norse village that has grown up around a spring. Walking down Keld Lane, the first building on the left is a stone chapel of great antiquity. Legend suggests that it is linked to Shap Abbey by an underground passage. The words 'flight' and 'fancy' immediately spring to mind when determining the efficacy of such a proposition.

At the bottom of the lane, keep on to cross the Lowther by the road bridge. Stretching away to the west, Rolfland Forest rises gradually in a series of untidy hummocks between the valleys of Wet Sleddale and Swindale. Barely a suggestion of tree growth remains today – only the rough, moorland wilderness inhabited by sheep and lost fell wanderers.

Turn left over a feeder rill to accompany the river upstream. The boundary of the National Park at this point follows the meandering course of the river around Brown Hill, but the route is virtually pathless as far as the stepping stones at Thornship.

Cross a reedy patch of grassland to stride over Thornship Gill, then forking into an old track that heads south-west across the shallow river terrace towards Steps Hall. Swing left to arrive at the river ford serving this isolated farmstead. Named after the set of stepping stones that span the broad reach, using them demands nerves of steel.

But have faith in your guide, and, of course, the original builders of this

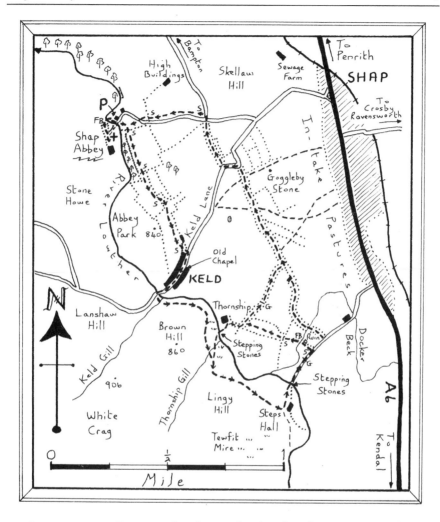

ancient causeway. It was not by chance that local pink granite was selected for the erection. Even on the wet day that found me at the point of no return, my boots held firm as the swirling torrent caressed the stalwart blocks.

Once the far shore is gained, walk up the lane for 150 metres to a stile on the left. Follow a broken wall down to cross Docker Beck using a solid footbridge. Another 50 metres will find you straddling another wall stile. Cross the next field to gain the abandoned access lane serving the farming hamlet of Thornship, one of the oldest hereabouts.

Bear right up the walled track, through a gate, then continue onwards to a T-junction. Here, take a left along the narrowing lane to its terminus at Keld Lane. Look out for the Goggleby Stone in a field on the right. Largest of the standing stones in the vicinity, it once formed part of an avenue which culminated in the arcane Thunder Stone located just beyond High Buildings. The significance of these relics from a bygone age suggests they were a potent force, influencing the lives of simple country folk. And in keeping with all such monoliths, a mystical allure surrounds their purpose.

Turn left down the lane towards Keld for 100 metres before slanting right to resume the walled path. Initially, it appears to enter a field. But do not be detoured, nor indeed deterred from taking the concealed route forking left of the opening. Scrabbling lianas from prickly thorn bushes attempt to hinder onward progress by plucking at exposed portions of flesh. Fend them off with a spirited ardour as you continue along to join the Bampton Road.

Cross over the access road down to the abbey and mount a stile to gain the far side of the wall. Accompany this down past High Buildings to the end of the field and over an exit stile. Descend the open grass fellside overlooking the Lowther Valley, crossing the road to return to the English Heritage car park at the bottom.

Far removed from the schedule of most Lakeland visitors, the short circuit of the Upper Lowther basin is steeped in mystery and imagination. The monks of Shap Abbey would have been pleased to note that the village enjoys virtually full employment due to the presence of British Steel, various quarries, and last but not least, a sausage factory.

Walk 2

Kirkby Stephen: A Bridge Too Far

Mysteries:	Stenkrith Bridge GR 773075 and New Bridge GR 774095
Distance:	5½ miles
Total Height Climbed:	Insignificant
Nearest Centre:	Kirkby Stephen
Start and Finish:	Limited parking is available on the roadside on the B6259, close to Stenkrith Bridge, opposite the gate where this walk begins.
Map:	Ordnance Survey Pathfinder 607, Tebay & Kirkby Stephen

Once regarded as a market town of excellence on account of the manufacture of high quality stockings, Kirkby Stephen possesses a colourful history stretching back to the mystifying Dark Ages. Of Norse origin, this 'farmstead with a church' was dedicated to Saint Stephen at a period when primitive gods of the new settlers were surrendering to Christian influences.

Built into the north wall of the parish church, the old Norse god Loki, chained and subdued, symbolised the curbing of the Devil's influence. Dating from the 10th century, this powerful entity exerted a mesmeric power over his primitive flock prior to the spread of Christianity. The stone once formed part of a cross akin to the specimen that still survives in the churchyard at Gosforth in West Cumbria.

Another occurrence that originated in Scandinavia involved the regular tolling of the church bell each evening around eight o'clock. Known as the Taggy Bell, it heralded a nightly curfew for children. Folk believed that Taggy lived on the fells and haunted the lanes during the hours of darkness, ready to pounce on those foolish enough to remain abroad at such an ungodly hour. Clearly, this would have been an effective means of keeping an eye on children before its demise at the end of the 19th century.

Our walk begins at Stenkrith Bridge, a narrow arch spanning the magnificent gorge carved out of the underlying bedrock by the River Eden. Built in 1764, the sight which confronted early travellers must have been awesome indeed. For here it is that the ancient river has discarded any benevo-

Stenkrith Bridge, where the Devil grinds mustard

lent aspirations it might have harboured in pursuit of a super-macho image.

Pummelling the bockram into submission, the churning cascade has chiselled the base rock out to form an abstract sculpture of impressive dimensions. Stepped layers of grey limestone, fluted and smooth, enable the ordinary walker to enter the very heart of the ravine whilst rushing torrents hiss and foam amid the split fissures.

At one with such a dynamic landscape, is it any wonder that tales associated with dark forces have arisen in this heady atmosphere? Known as the Devil's Mustard Mill, the rumblings that emanate from deep within the bowels of this magical rock garden have Old Nick's stamp upon them. People thought the wily fox came here to grind and mix the hot condiment to suit his fiery taste.

But as the age of enlightenment dawned, Stenkrith began to assume a more romantic façade and young lovers came to plight their troth. Certainly it is a bewitching locale, a captivating and winsome point from which to commence a circuit of this ancient market town.

The Walk

After passing through the gate on the east side of the B6259, immediately opposite where you have parked, take full advantage of the opportunity to explore the mysterious environs of this spectacular gorge. There is no other limestone scenery quite like it.

Then make your way along the grassy path, following the tree-lined river bank. Beyond a fence stile, accompany another fence round to a stile giving access to a rough, enclosed lane. This is where the river used to be forded in far off times, before Stenkrith Bridge was erected. Walkers are now provided with a substantial footbridge. Our route lies to the left, away from the river and up the lane which winds round to merge with the B6259 at the southern edge of Kirkby Stephen.

Head north into the town, bearing left to join the main street. At times, the negotiation of this busy thoroughfare can pose a distinct hazard to health and your continued intake of oxygen. As the principal route serving Cumbria from east of the Pennines, traffic congestion is threatening the peace and quiet of the town.

Expect, therefore, to see numerous leaflets campaigning for a by-pass as you proceed south, making a right turn down the first side road. Then it's left along Faraday Road, which parallels the main highway for 100 metres, before branching right up West Garth Avenue.

When this cul-de-sac narrows to a rough track, maintain a westward course between hedged ranks until it swings sharply to the left. Here cross a stile into a field and head north alongside a fence bounding the rugby ground. Cross a fence stile and go behind the high school, continuing towards the far right corner to pass through a gate.

Turn immediately left once again, heading west away from the town. Avoid the obvious field access lane forking left. Instead, make for a stile ahead to mount the facing grass bank with a fence on your right. On reaching a fenced corridor, enter it through a gate and descend to another at the bottom of the gentle cant.

At the corner of a wall, enter the next field by a stile and head directly for Sandwath Farm. Enter the yard by a gate, passing between the array of buildings and so down an access track to a back lane. Bear right to join another lane and then right again back towards Kirkby Stephen. After crossing How Gill, take note of the oddity created by a wall bridging the stream immediately behind the road bridge.

Fork left down a rough, enclosed lane immediately before the electricity sub-station. This track merges with yet another back lane feeding into the town. Head right and straight away left down the continuing right of way. Go straight over the walkers' crossroads. No need to look both ways here with lost woollies being the only traffic hazard likely to be encountered.

On reaching the Appleby Road, head right to gain the main A685 north of Kirkby Stephen where it crosses the Eden via New Bridge. Having replaced the original structure of 1649, it is debatable as to whether the dobbie who lurked beneath is still in residence. Known as Jingling Annas, he caused trouble for those travellers brave enough to use the road after dark.

Continued harassment led to curtailment of his dubious activities when a priest was called in to exorcise the spirit until the final call to retribution. Another theory is that the Wise Man of Stainmore appropriated the essence of the dobbie's being and secreted it beneath a stone close to the bridge. But which one? That is the burning question.

Cross to the far side of the bridge and through a stile to drop down to the riverside, which is carpeted with daffodils in spring. Beyond another fence stile, take a stroll south along the clear path inside a field fence. After another stile the path continues onward to Lowmill Bridge. Leave the road adjacent to the mill, crossing Hartley Beck by a short footbridge.

The main built-up area of the town lies at the top of a ridge on the right which drops steeply to the river below and is unseen from above. Indeed, the casual visitor will have no idea that a river plays such an important part in the siting of the town.

The right of way passes by the cricket pavilion, though not over the pitch itself, to reach the river walk at Frank's Bridge. This stone footbridge provides access to the river from the town centre, the stroll along the river being popular with locals on a fine afternoon, and rightly so. With sun dappling the water's edge and irrepressible flyers chirruping and cavorting, there can be few more tranquil sites for young and old alike to pass a languid hour.

Heading east, stick with the river to a fence stile. Leave the paved route which mounts the easy slope of Castle Hill alongside a wall, and swing right across an open field but still chaperoning the river. Pass right of a substantial barn to enter a wooded enclave at the point where Ladthwaite Beck ends with the River Eden.

Make use of the footbridge to gain the far bank, climbing up through the verdant screen with a disintegrating wall on the left. Head south-south-west along a fenced causeway which forks into another after 300 metres. Ford a minor stream to maintain a course paralleling the river, and cross the abandoned railway cutting by a preserved stone bridge. Many railway branch lines have been dismantled hereabouts. Where a network once criss-crossed the area, only the picturesque Settle-Carlisle is still in service.

Stick with the fenced track which fords Broad In Sike just north of Nateby village. After joining the B6259, head right for a half mile back to Stenkrith. This time make a detour along the river path on the left to view the Devil's Mustard Mill from the other side of the bridge.

Huge, cylindrical hollows have been scoured out by the swirling motion of pebbles wearing away at the porous limestone. The resultant patterns of geometric complexity were once thought to have been cauldrons utilised by Druid priests in pursuit of their sacrificial rites, the cloistered site appearing ideal for a Druid temple.

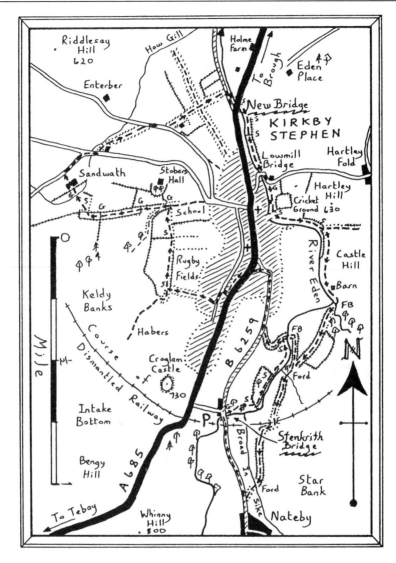

Such tales seek to further promote the sense of mystery and antiquity that envelops this special locality. Bridged at either end by structures that possess their own inimitable gleanings, the circuit of Kirkby Stephen enables one to take stock of past associations whilst engaging in a congenial ramble.

Walk 3

Cockermouth: Hang on to your Head!

Mystery:	The Executioner's Grave GR 086309
Distance:	5 miles
Total Height Climbed:	Insignificant
Nearest Centre:	Papcastle
Start and Finish:	After turning off the A66 towards Great Broughton, ample parking space is available on the left, immediately beyond Broughton High Bridge.
Map:	Ordnance Survey Pathfinder 575, Cockermouth and Maryport

In company with many early churches, the Norman edifice at Brigham near Cockermouth is removed at some distance from the village itself. Surrounded as it is by a substantial graveyard, could it be that the villagers were loath to become too closely acquainted with the permanent residents. If the coming fable strikes a memorable chord, this supposition will have been amply confirmed.

Ghosts flitting tenuously betwixt the grey tombstones are apt to drive a chilled ripple of trepidation down the spine of those venturing into such places. And never more so than when the spectre in question pursued a somewhat dubious profession – for Joseph Wilson, who came to haunt the Brigham graveyard, was none other than the official Carlisle hangman. Many were the unfortunate recipients of his terminal ministrations before this authorised neck-stretcher met his own untimely demise.

Perhaps it was the manner of his passing that occasioned such a morbid fascination with his grave that gruesome souvenir hunters chipped bits off the tombstone. Thoroughly disillusioned with the strained relations his chosen calling engendered with the local populace, Wilson engineered his own personal quietus in dramatic fashion.

It was a cold, bleak November day in 1757 when the distraught rope handler made his own final walk. But for him it was to be the river's swirling tentacles that enfolded him within their dank embrace after he jumped from the Cocker Bridge. Such was his fame, or notoriety, among his contemporaries that the coiled noose embellishing the headstone soon disappeared.

For the next century his ghost is said to have haunted the graveyard, instilling terror into all who ventured there after dark. Had the invasion of his final resting place so incensed the poor chap that he determined to have his revenge? Who can say?

Eventually, in 1860, the resident incumbent decided that his petrified parishioners needed urgent appeasement if the congregation was to be upheld. He accordingly exhumed the bones of the hangman and took the skull to Wilson's old cottage, where two cloggers named Watson then lived. Future events seem to indicate that Joseph Wilson had at last found peace, no further reports of spectral ferment having been reported since.

Today the Brigham graveyard has become a substantial resting place for the deceased of this burgeoning settlement. But a search for the executioner's grave proved fruitless. Maybe you will have more success.

The Carlisle hangman was buried in Brigham graveyard

The Walk

Our walk begins on the north side of the A66, the main east-west link serving north Lakeland. A gap in the bridge parapet followed by a flight of stone steps will deposit you in the field adjoining the River Derwent. Walk back upstream to cross a stile, then continue along a fence to another.

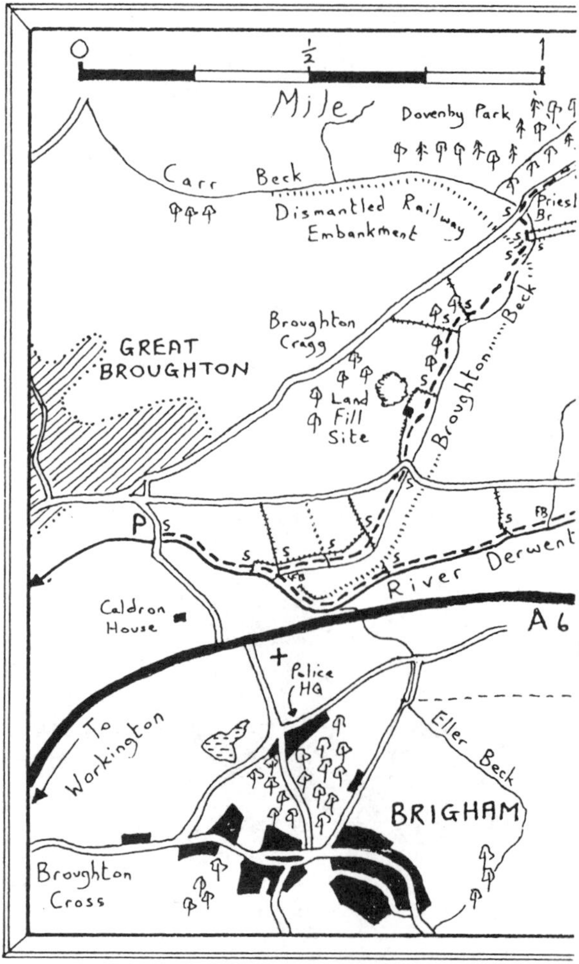

Here it is necessary to follow the left bank of Broughton Beck away from the Derwent, crossing two more stiles as the beck accompanies the old railway embankment. Arriving at a stepped wall stile, the Broughton road is joined. Take a left, proceed for 50 metres, then turn right up the access road serving a landfill site located in an old quarry.

Watch for an inconspicuous yellow waymarker on the right which points the way through the close-packed woodland which skirts the tortuous watercourse. After crossing two fence stiles, follow that on your right around to the stone pillars of the dismantled railway bridge.

Another stile allows access between the columns, after which a broken stile (September 1997) brings us to the broad beck terrace. Pick a course through the wanton growth of thistles to arrive at the next stile. A further 100 metres to the north will bring you to Priests Bridge.

Bear right up the road for 300 metres, until a public footpath sign appears on the right. This marks the course of the influential, arrow-straight Roman road connecting Alavna on the coast with Derwentio at Papcastle. Now completely obscured, it is difficult to imagine that this lonely trail once echoed to the steady tramp of legions marching between the two strongholds.

This section follows the only right of way that now exists. Cross the field to a corner, after which a narrow, wooded strip is negotiated with stiles at

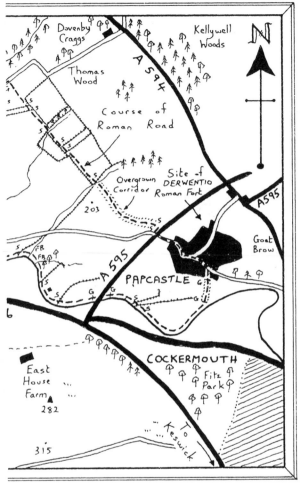

either end. Continue in a south-easterly direction for a half mile, alongside the field boundaries and passing over five more stiles. This will bring you to a fenced/hedged corridor.

Somewhat overgrown, a thin path can still be traced snaking through the welter of unbridled shrubbery and weeds. During summer, walkers in shorts are advised to protect their lower regions from the stinging onslaught of the deadly nettle that is profuse hereabouts. The middle phase of this corridor occupies a depressed culvert overhung with snarling branches.

At its termination, cross a stile leading immediately left to join another back road. Head left over the Cockermouth by-pass to enter the village of Papcastle. This distinctly odd name was proffered by early Norse settlers who found a hermit living amidst the bones of the Roman fort.

Nothing now remains of the strategic site that once draped the hill, extending all the way down to the river bank. Its stone walls were commandeered for the erection of Cockermouth Castle in the 14th century, now itself a ruined shell. Modern housing unfortunately appears to cover everything. Other forts such as the preserved specimen at Hard Knott were more providential, being remote from centres of population.

Take a stroll down the narrow main street of the village until a minor crossroads is reached. Here, bear right, soon passing through a gate to make your way down a rough-walled passage. Another gate at the end gives onto the river bank, which is followed downstream.

Around the first bend, cross two stiles and go under the by-pass where it straddles the river. At the time of writing two gates allowed onward progress, although a footpath diversion plans to alter the course slightly. Continuing along the river's edge, the hum of traffic from the A66 is never far away. Beyond a fence stile, pass a distinctive green hut used by local anglers.

After the next stile, cross two footbridges, which will bring you to a steeply undercut banking on a sharp bend in the river. Ascend the incline through the tree cover to cross a stile at the top edge. A footbridge soon after then leads down to the lower level once again beyond the next stile.

Another quarter mile and the path homes in to parallel the old railway embankment at another stile. Passing between dismantled bridge supports, the route ahead should be on the river side of the fence. Once the footbridge over Broughton Beck has been crossed, our outward route is rejoined back to Broughton High Bridge.

The mysteries regarding Derwentio fort and the hangman's grave would appear to centre on discovering visible evidence supporting their existence. Both have suffered from the ravages of later generations vandalising the sites, albeit for diverse reasons.

Walk 4

Appleby: Where There's a Will

Mystery:	Crackenthorpe Hall GR 662218
Special Requirements:	Bring a towel!
Distance:	5½ miles
Total Height Climbed:	Insignificant
Nearest Centre:	Long Marton
Start and Finish:	Park on the old road in the village of Crackenthorpe, on either side of the by-pass.
Map:	Ordnance Survey Pathfinder 578, Appleby-in-Westmorland

Slithering down the mid stretch of the Eden Valley like a giant python, the A66 now avoids the hamlet of Crackenthorpe. No doubt the residents have thanked their lucky stars, plus a host of worthy campaigners, for segregating them from this busy thoroughfare breaching the Pennine Chain.

Traffic bustling effortlessly along the by-pass will have little notion of the histrionic pageantry that has been played out behind the small cluster of woods to the south. Secreted within this verdant mantle, Crackenthorpe Hall stands silent and aloof from the passage of time. Moss-clad walls, sinister and brooding, issue a dash of latent mystery that one can almost reach out and touch.

Once a vibrant and lively household, this ancient seat of the Machells now lies gaunt and dejected, no longer pulsating with sounds of joy and laughter. It is a melancholic shadow of its former distinction. Turning its back on the modern world, the hall has still managed to retain that essential hint of past eccentricity that has contributed to its reputation as a haunted house of some renown.

And what tales this ancestral pile could doubtless relate. Even a king is known to have sheltered within the dour walls. For it was Henry VI who sought refuge at Crackenthorpe following his defeat by the Yorkists at Hexham in 1464. Being a keen gardener, he spent much of his sanctuary improving the floral semblance. One of the plots was thereafter known as The King's Garden.

One of the oldest families in Old Westmorland, the Machell dynasty finally came to an end when the last surviving member was killed at the

Battle of the Somme in 1915. Perhaps the most colourful episode, certainly the most bizarre, occurred some three centuries earlier. This was a period when the aristocratic Machells were staunch Royalists, supporting Charles I against the usurper Oliver Cromwell.

At this time, Lancelot Machell married a certain Elizabeth Sleddal, known as Peg. The pair lived happily at Crackenthorpe, enjoying a grand lifestyle even following Cromwell's victory. Upon her husband's sad passing, his will caused much indignation and Peg was exceedingly agitated by the stipulated contents. What exactly caused such disquiet has never been discovered.

Following her own demise, Peg's anger reached out from beyond the grave. She would often reappear to haunt the family home, causing succeeding generations a great deal of distress and consternation, especially leading members who were themselves close to the final shakedown.

Many became deranged with fearful terror, until finally it was decided to exhume Peg's remains and have them reburied where she could no longer cause trouble. A hole

The entrance to Crackenthorpe Hall, home of Peg Sleddal

was dug in the bed of the River Eden and a huge block of granite rolled over the hole. Performing the ceremony, the priest failed to make the exorcism absolute, thus allowing Peg to rise from her watery grave once every year.

Her favoured month is September, when she can often be seen making her way up to the King's Bedchamber at Crackenthorpe Hall. Local hearsay intimates that Peg only appears when the Helm Wind girds up to blast an earthy chorus down from the heights around Fiends Fell. Uttering a frenetic howl of wrath, the fervid gust accompanies Peg in a coach pulled by six black horses.

And such is the link between them that it is said the Helm only blows when Peg's temper erupts with fiery passion. Other visitations can be of a more sombre mode, suggesting that Peg Sleddal sometimes regrets the curse she placed on the Machell name. On occasion, she has been seen crying beneath an oak tree close by Crackenthorpe Hall. Her tears are thought to precede a misfortune in the family that cheated her all those years ago.

The Walk

After passing the entrance to the hall, head south past the cement works to the first bungalow on the left, Homelea. Cross a wall stile into the garden of Lorna and David Graham, who run a holiday home for handicapped children. A laudable calling which has tempered their attitude to walkers, who are permitted to use their property to unofficially reach a field behind. The official right of way is impossible to use since the cement works erected a high concrete barrier, and it is to the Graham's credit that they allow us to use their garden. Say hello to the numerous guinea pigs you encounter en route.

Across the back field, another stile gives on to the short but steep banking up to the main road. Cross straight over with care, and through an obscured stile into the field on the far side. Head half right to parallel a fence up to a gate at the far end.

Continue ahead up a shallow rise, aiming for a gap in a wall of concrete pillars. Narrow in the extreme, it will be necessary to divest your rucksack in order to squeeze through. Those of a more portly stature should breathe deeply and trust to luck.

On the right, Roger Head appears to be a farm dedicated to the breeding of horses, which are apt to regard walkers as dispensers of tasty titbits. Expect a retinue of followers around the small copse behind the farm up to the next stile. Beware a shocking jolt from the electric fence immediately after the stile. Stepping over it in a cautious manner will assuredly benefit vital appendages.

Follow the fence on your right over three more stiles, the last slightly offset in the adjoining field, to gain the Roman road. Straight as a snooker cue, these well-engineered highways march effortlessly across the countryside, deviating from a direct course only to avoid major obstacles – of which there are none in this part of the Eden Valley.

Cross to the far side over a stile and go along a hedge to Castrigg. An abrupt left then right through a gate passes left of the house and so reaches a fence. Beyond the stile, drop down to another located 100 metres ahead. Here it is necessary to slant left along a line of hawthorns to reach a farm track. Stick close to the fence for 100 metres, merging with the lane through a gate.

Head north-west along this old link serving the farms of this side of Keld Sike. Three gates and a stile followed by another stile will bring you into the farmyard of Far Broom, which specialises in pig breeding. Accompany the farm access road up to a metalled highway where a right is taken as far as Church House.

Immediately after passing the house, take the stiled footpath, following the wall on your left to cross Keld Sike by a footbridge. Head half-left across the next field, up to a line of trees. Over the fence stile, drop down to accompany Trout Beck along to the road.

Make a left here to enter the outskirts of Long Marton. Veer left along an unmade back lane. Unless curiosity wins the day, there is little to detain us in this small village so take the first left along the edge of a new housing estate. Fork left at Hawthorn Cottage down a hedged track. After passing through a gate, follow the fence on your right in a left swing round to a small copse. A field access track shears off to the right.

Entering a fenced corridor over a stile, the path loops to the right through a gate then goes along a straight section to another gate, where a sconce of trees rises up on the right. Another gate follows after 200 metres, beyond which is still another. Slant immediately left after passing through this and follow a fence to arrive at Trout Beck.

And this, ladies and gentlemen, is where a vital decision has to be made.
As the right of way leaps across the trundling stream, mere humans are obliged to discard boots and socks in order to wade across if the direct course is chosen. There is no footbridge (September 1997), hence the need for a towel.

But there is an alternative should the expected crossing facility not have materialised prior to your arrival. Head left for 300 metres until a bridging point is reached. This involves a log stretched across the channel, complete with a steel cable to assist balance. Return along the opposite bank to continue the walk on the right of a fence up to Powis House.

Cross a stile, making your way to the right through the maze of farm buildings and then along the access road to a back lane. Directly opposite the farm entrance, join the Roman road to head south-east in a direct line.

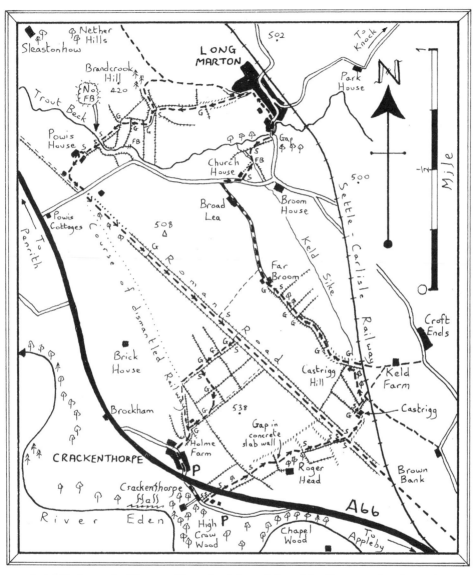

Initially bounded by a wall on the left and the old railway embankment on the right, the way soon becomes enclosed by trees.

Stick with it for a half mile before passing through a gate. Continue ahead on the path that disciplined ranks of tramping legions stamped out almost two millennia ago, in the early dawn of civilisation. Another half mile will bring you to a further gate. Immediately after this one, mount a stile on the right and walk up a shallow rise alongside the fence on your left.

Two gates and a quarter mile further, watch for a double stile on the left. Cross over these, and take a stroll along the hedge to the next field. There, make a diagonal crossing to the opposite corner on a clear field track which then crosses the old dismantled railway, barely noticeable as such hereabouts. Walk down the track to the last gate, which gives on to a rough T-junction.

Bear left here to arrive at Crackenthorpe through the back door. Turn left down the village street, quiet and traffic free since it was by-passed, to return from whence you came.

And should the Helm Wind choose to stir up a baying lament, do not be surprised to witness a coach and six sweeping out from the secluded entrance to Crackenthorpe Hall with Peg Sleddal in the driving seat.

Walk 5

Shap: Carved in Stone

Mysteries:	Crosby Hall GR 620149, The Garden of Images GR 604176, Meaburn Hall GR 624171
Distance:	5½ miles
Total Height Climbed:	Insignificant
Nearest Centre:	Crosby Ravensworth
Start and Finish:	Park on the wide verge adjacent to Dalebanks Beck in the village of Crosby Ravensworth, 50 metres beyond Haberwain Lane.
Map:	Ordnance Survey Pathfinder 597, Crosby Ravensworth and Brough

Located barely three miles from the M6 and Shap, the rural backwater of the Lyvennet Valley, a tributary of the mighty Eden, appears to have been sidetracked by commercial progress. Little has changed here in centuries and the tiny villages scattered throughout the region remain unspoilt and remote from the normal tourist itinerary.

Few outsiders venture along the narrow byways. Only those who have lost their way or other owners of this book are likely to be encountered along the intermittent paths. Such lonely territory has encouraged the appearance of strange phenomena, from which has emerged a trio of colourful happenings to satisfy the most jaded palate.

Removed from traffic interference, a natural silence enfolds the landscape, broken only by the occasional cawing of birds and the bleat of sheep. Truly an idyllic locale to savour and enjoy at one's leisure.

The Garden of Images at Reagill

The Walk

Begin by strolling up the road towards the church and crossing Dalebanks Beck via a set of large stepping stones concealed in the reeds. Walk up the track serving Crosby Hall, a plain and rather austere abode that harbours a ghost of the most malicious persuasion.

Reputed to have been the spirit of a former owner of the hall who was murdered, the spectre frequently took the form of a great white bull. The creature would slap and lick the windows with spiteful vigour, delighting in the fear engendered in the occupants.

Another caustic trick of the ghost was to shake the tower adjoining the main building until its bell chimed out a lusty chorus, which struck terror into the hearts of all the villagers. Such was the strength of fear generated by this odious spectre that in the early 19th century the tower was demolished.

Taking pity on the deranged farmer, the bull disclosed the location of a long abandoned treasure trove. It also accurately predicted the fellow's final removal from this mortal coil, but was then never seen again. So if the windows of Crosby Hall appear a trifle on the dirty side, blame should be laid squarely at the feet of the white bull.

And if any such quadruped is sighted as you pass left of the main building and through the gate at the far end, give him an extra wide berth. You never know. The virulent dobbie might well have returned and we do not want to ring down the curtain on this splendid walk before it has even begun.

Hurry around to the left, then circle right up a shallow incline to pass through a fenced gate ahead. Aim for the telegraph pole in the middle of the field and then across to the far left corner. Here it is necessary to make a double stile crossing of the field angle. Slant diagonally over the next field, keeping left of the stone building at the far side.

A wall stile gives access to the rough garden pasture that was once part of ruined Crake Trees. Another stile in the wall on the left is followed soon after by another at the top right corner of this small enclosure. At this point, bear right, heading north along the edge of the field.

Many of the fields hereabouts are planted with growing crops in the summer months, making paths sketchy or non-existent. You will need to plough through an ocean of wheat (July '97), which can leave you a little on the damp side after rain. But around the field boundaries, stiles have been well maintained, no doubt in anticipation of an influx of ghost hunters clutching a GKD mysterious guide.

Maintain a straight course north over two more stiles, which will bring you to a large field. Follow the right-hand edge for about 100 metres before crossing to the far side and over another stile. Drop down a grassy bank and

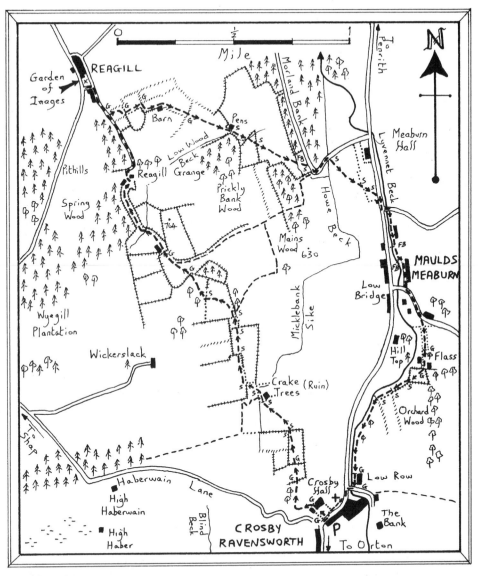

then stroll across to a fence gate. Stride over this field and fork into a clear track that passes a pair of sheep processing sheds en route to Reagill Grange.

The fenced track accompanies the extensive plantation of Spring Wood on the left. Reagill Grange is impressive on account of its profusion of circular chimneys. Look to see if the dobbie stone still hangs near the main door. Round with a hole in it, giving the appearance of a polo mint, the stone was intended to ward off any rampant spirits that might have harboured mischief towards the inhabitants.

Beyond the grange, join the access road and then continue ahead to Reagill itself. Take the first road on the left and peer over a stone wall on your right. Here you will gain a taster of what the celebrated Garden of Images has to offer. The current owners of the farm have made an effort to keep this peerless sward tidy. They are a friendly crew who should raise no objections to your viewing the curiosity at close quarters. But knock and pass the time of day first.

Created through the artistic talent of Thomas Bland, this lowly farmer achieved recognition by chiselling and carving a veritable cornucopia of sculptures around the middle of the 19th century. From knights to nobles, dogs to devils, effigies wrought in stone make the garden a unique feature without equal anywhere else in Cumbria. Also a prolific artist, his prowess with brush and canvas has unfortunately been lost to posterity.

The Garden of Images became a cultural vision included in the annual festival held by Thomas Bland in honour of Queen Victoria. Poetry, music and dancing were enjoyed by guests clad in fancy dress, all of which added to the surreal atmosphere that such an assemblage must have inspired.

Other sculptures have been attributed to Thomas Bland, the strangest perhaps being that erected close to the source of the Lyvennet Beck at a remote spot above Crosby Ravensworth known as Black Dub. It commemorates the place where Charles II rested his army in 1651 during a futile attempt to regain control of the English throne from Oliver Cromwell.

Perhaps it was the bizarre nature of Bland's creations that encouraged a darker aspect to infiltrate the settlement of Reagill. Villagers often caught sight of a lady dressed all in white, and at what other time but during the hours of darkness. Major White (no pun intended) saw what he believed to be a white owl in a tree whilst out horse riding. He drew his pistol and immediately shot the apparition, which swelled to form the White Lady herself. She jumped up behind him, so terrifying the major's horse that it bolted in a fit of madness. Through hedges and shrubbery, the lathered mount careered onward. When at last it deposited the luckless fellow at his home, his once resplendent finery hung in tatters from a bleeding torso.

The distraught major never fully recovered from this debilitating experience. And one can only speculate as to whether a change of name would have expedited his recovery.

Head back down the road towards Reagill Grange, taking the signposted track to Maulds Meaburn. After 50 metres, the track swings to the right to pass through a gate, continuing alongside a wall on your right. After the next gate, lean immediately right and follow the edge of the field to an old barn.

After this, swing right to chaperone a hedge and then go through a small gate. Our way now descends easy grass slopes into the valley bottom, where you should aim for the left corner of Prickly Bank Wood and some fenced sheep pens. A wall stile is hidden until the last minute, after which we circle round to the right through a fence gate.

Cross the field to a stile located midway along the next fence. Maintain a straight course, heading south-west past the edge of Mains Wood to ford a narrow gill by means of a footbridge. A stile then gives access to the Morland Bank road which scythes through the massed sconce of conifers.

The road then veers sharply to the left, crossing Howe Beck. Immediately over the bridge, enter a field heading south-east to fork into the substantial wall enclosing Meaburn Hall. Solid and unyielding, the roughcast exterior conceals a dire secret that has never been laid to rest.

Being the earliest seat of the Lowther family, it is said that two brothers fought a duel in one of the first floor rooms. Neither gained the upper hand. But even when the fight was called off, they were unable to settle their differences in an amicable manner. To avoid further discomfiture for the family, both men left the hall never to be seen again.

What lurks behind the sinister walls of Meaburn Hall?

From that time until fairly recently, the infamous room was sealed up. Blanketed in secrecy, the hidden chamber caused a dark cloud to hang over the hall, creating a fetid air of hostility. Even today, one can sense the brooding atmosphere that hangs in the air surrounding Meaburn Hall.

Beyond a wall stile, drop down to gain the back lane close to a lone cottage. Walk back up the lane for 200 metres if you wish to become more acquainted Meaburn's ghostly past. Thereafter, head south for 100 metres to cross over Low Bridge, spanning Lyvennet Beck, and then immediately right along an access road serving a row of cottages at this northern end of Maulds Meaburn.

When the paved section ends, follow a grass track alongside the beck until it merges with another service road. Pass a line of houses on this eastern side of the dispersed village which straddles this major tributary of the River Eden.

Join a lane at the far end and head left towards the Appleby road. Break from this after 200 metres down the road serving Flass. This imposing abode hidden amongst the trees is well past its heyday as a stately home. Ignore the first track branching left. A little further along, pass to the left of the main entrance to Flass through a small gate.

At the end of a tree-covered boundary wall, go under a low-arched tunnel to enter an open field by a gate. Bear half right to the far corner and through a stile to parallel Lyvennet Beck. Accompany this all the way round to Low Row, where a pair of substantial gates at either end of a lawned concourse will deposit you in a back lane.

Take a right over the beck bridge to pass the old church of Crosby Ravensworth on your way back to the car. A trio of contrasting mysteries that leave much to contemplate, and a walk that is equally appealing for the charm and serenity prevalent in the beautiful Lyvennet Valley – there could be no more appropriate conclusion.

Walk 6

Penrith: An Illustrious Past

Mysteries:	The Noble Shepherd GR 537290, King Arthur's Round Table GR 523284, Skulduggery GR 528284
Distance:	6½ miles
Total Height Climbed:	Negligible
Nearest Centre:	Eamont Bridge
Start and Finish:	Park on the grass verge along the side road off the A66, adjacent to the site of Brocavum.
Map:	Ordnance Survey English Lakes, 1:25 000, north-east area

Gaunt and forbidding, the red sandstone walls of Brougham Castle stand as a reminder of the grim realities of life in medieval Cumbria. Now but a decaying remnant of its former glory, the strategic site at the confluence of the Rivers Eamont and Lowther was essential to combat the covetous aspirations of warmongers, who were a constant threat.

Most renowned of the families that occupied Brougham Castle during its turbulent history were the Cliffords. They ruled the surrounding territory with an iron fist for three centuries. One old story concerns a certain Lady Clifford who was determined to save the lives of her two sons following an ignominious defeat of the favoured Lancastrians at the Battle of Towton in 1461. The youngest she sent abroad, but it was Henry, the eldest and heir to the vast Clifford estates, who was most in danger.

A trusted friend arranged for the youngster to live with a childless shepherd and his wife near Threlkeld. During the following years, Henry was raised as if he were their own and adopted the humble rustic life with alacrity. Becoming skilled in country pursuits, he grew into an intelligent lad but never learned to read or write.

Although Lady Clifford kept a maternal eye on Henry, he never learned of his true identity until the Tudor dynasty assumed the throne of England in 1485. When presented at the court of King Henry VII, the young man shocked the assembled dignitaries with his homespun simplicity. Lacking the refinement of his regal contemporaries, Henry nonetheless proved his birthright in a heavy Cumbrian dialect that endeared him to the king, who allowed him to return to Brougham as Lord of the Manor.

Although he always favoured an outdoor life to the opulent grandeur of his aristocratic heritage, the Shepherd Lord was an able leader, admired and respected by all his tenants. Barden Tower in Wharfedale became his preferred home, where he lived simply until a peaceful death took him at the age of seventy.

Most eminent of all the Cliffords was Lady Anne. Single-minded and assiduous in her efforts to restore family pride in the 17th century, she managed the estate business with detailed efficiency. Her dogmatic persistence complemented a generosity which can be illustrated in a quaint occurrence concerning the lawsuit issued against a Huddersfield clothier. Having won her case regarding payment of a 'boon hen', the good lady invited her opponent to dinner and proceeded to serve up the said fowl on a golden platter.

Following the demise of the venerable countess, the name of Clifford ceased to echo through the vaulted chambers. And so after thirteen generations of continuous occupancy, Brougham Castle was finally abandoned to the elements.

Prior to setting out on this historic pilgrimage, take note of the ancient earthworks secreted over the wall on your left. Grassed over and the preserve of grazing sheep, only the basic outline of Brocavum Fort can be made out today. The Romans were quick to recognise the importance of the site as a focus of routes. In consequence, a key fort was erected at the eastern end of the High Street where a thousand soldiers were garrisoned.

Brougham Castle: home to the Cliffords, but now a preserved ruin

The Walk

Walk down the lane, making the time to visit and imbibe the heady atmosphere emanating from the crumbling façade of Brougham Castle. In view of its role at the crux of a transit network, Brougham has never been a remote outpost. Traffic might have been a tad more sedate in those far off days, but the ease of communication with the rest of the country was doubtless welcomed by the inhabitants.

Cross the bridge spanning the River Eamont and branch right down a short lane immediately before reaching the main road. Cross the fence stile on your left to make your way across the open pasture to the river bank. After heavy rain it is apparent that these fields are prone to flooding. Perhaps a brief call to the local weather centre would be wise before setting off from home if you are unsure.

Head west alongside the river, proceeding upstream towards Eamont Bridge. Cross two stiles, sticking close to the river all the way around the sweeping meander until a sconce of enclosed woodland is reached at the far side of Carltonhall Park. The large building on the right is Carlton Hall, headquarters of Cumbria Constabulary.

Enter the woods over a ladder stile and slant half right away from the river. Merge with a fenced corridor, at the end of which is a stile sited close to the edge of the thin, wooded strip. Over the stile, bear immediately left to mount another, then head right along a wide track to Eamont Bridge. Take a left over the River Eamont Bridge to stroll along the village street, which is the A6! At its junction with the B5232, a pair of inns endeavour to tempt you in with enticing offers.

On the right is to be found a raised circular dais approximating to 100 metres in diameter. Originating from around 2000BC, it is thought to have been a Bronze Age burial site and meeting place. Some years later, 2500 to be precise, it is possible that the legendary King Arthur gathered here with his knights of the round table.

Historians assert that games were played here in medieval times with the spectators ranged around the perimeter, seated on the surrounding banks. A vivid imagination is required to conjure up these ancient sportsmen and their audience.

If the struggle proves too great, especially if you have tarried awhile in either of the adjacent pubs, continue south to cross Lowther Bridge. Then take a left along the B6262 to Brougham Hall. Opposite the imposing walls stands the 14th-century church renovated by Lady Anne Clifford in 1649, wherein are interred generations of Broughams.

Today the hall is but a ruined shell undergoing extensive refurbishment. Craft workshops have been opened and it is intended to have a substantial museum eventually. The outer walls are largely intact, including the august medieval gatehouse. With a chequered history stretching back into an obscure past, the legend of the Brougham Skull offers a bewitching turn of events that actually ended happily.

It concerns a human skull that was kept on display inside the hall for generations. Such a gruesome artefact was seldom viewed with equanimity. Once, it was thrown out on a dung heap, whereupon ill-fortune befell the inhabitants until it was reinstated. As with all such bizarre happenings, night-time was when torment and spectral disturbance was at its height.

Whenever the skull was removed, haunting and fearful noises invaded the property. And each time the grinning skull came home, peace and harmony also returned. Always on view, it was not the most appealing sight to welcome guests into the hall. There appeared to be no answer to the problem until it was suggested that the grimacing ogre should be bricked up inside the walls. Inside the building, yet out of sight. And so it came to pass that the curse of the skull was finally bested.

Take your leave of Brougham Hall by turning right off the secondary road into a new housing development then immediately left. The right of way cuts across the corner of a garden then follows the back fence. After 50 metres, it enters a fenced corridor that circles right behind the houses as far as a stretch of woodland.

Cross a stile to enter a large field and then accompany the fenced edge of the tree line. When it swings to the right, forge ahead across the broad tract of Broughamhall Park, aiming for an arch in the wall ahead. After passing through an incongruous, steel-barred gate, head south along the A6 for a half mile to the village of Clifton.

Poking above the farm buildings of Clifton Hall, a squat pele tower commands attention. Smaller than many other such relics scattered throughout Cumbria, its crenellated battlements have been well preserved. Likened to the log cabins of frontier America, the peles remind Cumbrians of their tempestuous heritage, when isolated communities needed protection from violent predators.

The village also marks the site of the last battle fought on English soil during the Jacobite rebellion of 1745. Bonnie Prince Charlie's retreating Scot's army put up a spirited resistance when attacked by the Duke of Cumberland. Although the result was inconclusive, both factions claimed a victory on that gloomy November day.

Opposite Clifton Hall stands the old stone church dedicated to St Cuthbert. Monks rested here whilst carrying the body of the saint to its final resting place. The church erected on the site makes for a fitting memorial.

Continue along the main street of this linear village for another quarter mile, taking the left turn signposted to Clifton Dykes. Two hundred metres after crossing the railway line, the hedged track swings sharply to the right.

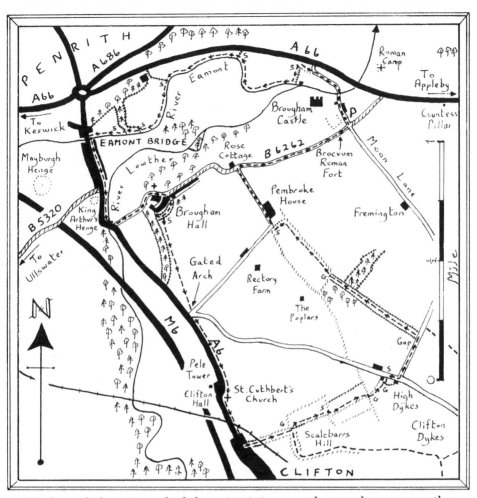

Go through the gate on the left, maintaining a north-easterly course on the left side of a hedge over Scalebarrs Hill. At the end of the field, cross a stile and carry on along the right-hand edge of the next field.

Pass through a gate adjacent to a wooden hen house with the hedge now on the left. Continue ahead to High Dykes. Beyond the next gate the path passes to the right of a covered sheep pen and then through a wall gap to arrive at a lane. Turn right for 50 metres and then left down Moon Lane.

Strolling down here, the mighty wall of the Pennine Chain controls the eastern horizon with Cross Fell holding centre stage. Highest point along England's sturdy backbone, the eye is inevitably drawn to the white-domed weather centre atop Great Dun Fell. Make a point of visiting this most fiendish of fell tops on Walk 27.

Watch out for a gap on the left after 300 metres which marks the start of an arrow-straight, fenced causeway across the fields to Pembroke House. Initially flanked by young conifers, the causeway passes left of an established belt of conifers as it forges across the flat, grassy plain. Take heed of clutching spiny tendrils that make querulous attempts to hinder progress.

On reaching a gate the track becomes wider and easier, proceeding directly to Pembroke House with a hedge on the right. Bear left along the wall bounding the first property to cross a stile. Walk down the lane past Pembroke, noting the Church of St Paul located inside a barn on the right.

At the T-junction opposite Rose Cottage, take a right for a half mile back to the crossroads adjacent to Brocavum Fort. This walk takes in a broad array of ancient structures and artefacts within the compass of the Brougham estates. Historical fact and folklore blend together, embracing the breadth of human endeavour within this engaging locale.

Walk 7

Pooley Bridge: An Ancient Pedigree

Mysteries:	Baron's Hill GR 475283, The Four Bears GR 460266, Dacre Castle GR 461265
Distance:	4½ miles
Total Height Climbed:	100 feet (30 metres)
Nearest Centre:	Stainton
Start and Finish:	Approaching Baron's Hill along the A66, turn down into Stainton. Take a right turn at the village crossroads and park up this cul-de-sac.
Map:	Ordnance Survey English Lakes, 1:25 000, north-east area

Tucked away on the north-east fringe just outside the Lake District National Park boundary, Stainton exudes an air of affluence and modernity. The old core of the village is easily missed, being secreted amongst a sprawl of contemporary villas. Lying close to the M6 junction has made it ideally placed for commuting to Carlisle and Penrith.

Nobody would imagine that lowly Stainton once boasted a church or even an abbey of august proportions, where human bones have been unearthed amongst the ruins. And herein lies a story concerning a certain landowner of infamous repute. The raffish tyrant governed his tenants with a rasping severity that was to cost him dear. This was at the time when the established church was in dire straits occasioned by the matrimonial problems of Henry VIII.

The noble in question hired men to strip the church down to its foundations in order to build himself a fitting domicile. After one particular visit, he rode off in a westerly direction. On cresting the first hillock, he looked back to the ruins he had created and was immediately thrown from his horse.

A broken neck was the price that the scurvy knave had to pay for his desecration of God's house. And to this day, the spectral figure of a galloping rider is occasionally spotted on the rise known as Baron's Hill.

The Walk

The sleepy village itself nowadays possesses little of interest, so walk up to the end of the lane and take the right fork. Entering a pinched corridor, ini-

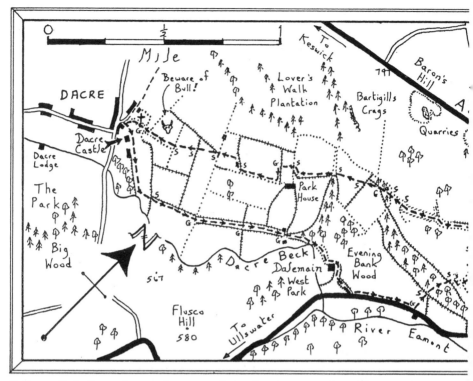

tially walled, the path soon becomes fenced as it passes through an arched tunnel of leafy boughs. The National Park is entered soon after passing a walled junction.

Continue ahead, crossing a stile with a wall on a rising bank to the right. Another 100 metres and the path enters the spindly confines of Evening Bank Wood, an elongated belt of woodland having the shape of a pirate's cutlass. All too soon we are out of the far side, where a gate gives on to the open field.

Cross a fence stile into the next field and aim half left down the facing grassy sward to the stiled gap in the line of trees at the far side. Then follow a fence on your left down to another bank of trees. Occasional matured oaks stand watch along the route. A rustic complement to the open prospect towards the head of Ullswater.

Bear right along the trees to cross a stile, then go over the next field to a fence, there to pass through a gate hidden until the last minute. Here the right of way has been diverted down the wall to the edge of the field close to Park House. Follow the wall around to the next fence.

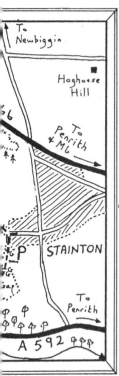

Beyond this stile, slant right to rejoin the original course of the path, following a direct course to the south-west. Negotiating three further stiles will bring you to the boundary of a large field on the far side of the grassy dome known as Loudon Hill. Stroll down the easy gradient with a wall on your left. But keep a wary eye open for the horny beast that often roams this pasture. And bully for you should this warning go unheeded.

Pass through a gate to enter the well-kept graveyard of St Andrew's parish church. Here is to be found one of the most intriguing mysteries in the neighbourhood. First identify the positions of The Four Bears. To the uninitiated, mere lumps of oddly carved stone.

But the enigmatic tale surrounding them will tax the grey matter of the most circumspect investigator. Little is known of their origin except that they appear to be a mischievous form of medieval strip cartoon and are thought to mark the limits of an old monastery.

Beginning at the north-west corner and moving anti-clockwise, the first bear is asleep with its head resting on a pillar. A cat then leaps on the bear's back. This is followed by a vigorous attempt to dislodge the interloper. And finally, the bear catches and eats its attacker. This interpretation was suggested by Chancellor Ferguson in 1890. Judge for yourself his reasoning. Puzzling, outlandish and even amusing, the Dacre Bears are positively unique.

Emerging from the churchyard, bear left down to the main village street, and immediately left again along the footpath signposted to Dalemain. Ahead the imposing bastion of Dacre Castle is all encompassing.

*One of the bears in St Andrew's graveyard
– but which one?*

The only free-standing pele tower that is still inhabited, the grim auster-
ity of the crenellated fortress has been tempered by an arboreous scarf
around its perimeter. This does nought to detract from the daunting sense
of antiquity pulsating through the thick walls of the grim stronghold. Home
of the Dacres, who controlled much of Cumbria in the Dark Ages, they suffered from a lack of male heirs to continue the family name.

Last in line, Thomas Dacre thought the family succession had been assured when his wife gave birth to a son after having delivered three girls.
His unfortunate partiality for local girls inevitably resulted in the arrival of
an illegitimate son. Not wishing to be associated with such an indiscretion,
he disavowed responsibility, whereupon the distraught girl threw herself
into Dacre Beck.

Her drowned body was found some days later. On learning of this ignominious affront to her daughter's honour, the mother immediately laid a
curse on the Dacre household. Extinction of the family name was brought
about as prophesied when Thomas's son fell from his rocking horse and
was killed. The roguish upstart himself received a visit from the Grim
Reaper soon after. At the moment of death, it was reputed that the ghostly
presence of the wronged maiden ceased her haunting of the meadows
around Dacre.

Our route passes under the grey portals of the castle, heading down towards Dacre Beck. After 200 metres, the clear track swings to the left alongside a fence, carving a direct course through the waving fields of ripening
wheat (Summer 1997). Funnelling into a high-walled back entry, the path
eventually reaches Dalemain. Hidden behind a protective skein of verdant
sentinels, this stately pile has been occupied by the Hassel family for 300
years and remains unseen until you arrive in the rear courtyard.

Even if your intention is to carry on, no resident ghost having been reported, make time to enjoy a well-earned cuppa in the original medieval
hall. Then follow the access road through the car park and round to the
main A592. Head left towards Penrith for about 300 metres, keeping well
into the narrow verge as there is no pavement.

On reaching the first building on the right, watch for an iron-barred gate
opposite. Cross to the far right corner of the field, where a fence stile allows
entry to the cloistered seclusion of Evening Bank Wood. A thin yet clear
path climbs the tree-clad slope to its far edge, which is guarded by a narrow
limestone scar.

Cross a fence stile and immediately on the right a stepped wall stile to
gain the adjacent field. Follow this wall round through a gap and so exit
from the National Park. Ahead, two gates close together provide a pen
which the local farmer utilises to hand shear the sheep in early summer.

Once shorn of their winter overcoat, the ungainly ewes totter away, glad to escape the indignity of being upended.

Should you be fortunate enough to observe this ancient yet essential craft, pay due heed to a dying art as most of the clipping is now done with electric shears. At one time the shearing season was a major social occasion, with much merrymaking and jollity enjoyed by all. Today, the low price of wool barely pays for the labour involved.

Having passed through the pen, cross the next field through a wide gap to a gate at the far side. The right of way passes through a private garden at this point to emerge on a back lane through a small wicket gate. A brief stroll down the lane will return you to the start.

Certainly there is much to occupy the mind on this historic foray into the remote pastures of north-east Lakeland. Ancient tradition and folklore go hand in hand with the churlish activities of those who should have known better. So what is your interpretation of The Dacre Bears?

Walk 8

Appleby: Of Trees and Vikings

Mysteries:	Orm the Viking GR 701177, Hilton's Sycamore GR 701176, Whitehead's Cedar GR 709168
Distance:	7 miles
Total Height Climbed:	Insignificant
Nearest Centre:	Great Ormside
Start and Finish:	Park on the grass verge at the north end of the main street in Great Ormside.
Map:	Ordnance Survey Pathfinder 597, Crosby Ravensworth & Brough

Two miles south of Appleby and tucked away on a bend of the River Eden, the village of Great Ormside presents the epitome of rural England. An ancient settlement of noble heritage, its pedigree stretches back into the mists of antiquity. It is generally believed that Viking invaders led by a fiery character named Orm settled in this fertile valley around AD915.

The church of St James stands proudly on a man-made dais, whereon was established a pagan burial ground prior to the settlers being converted to Christianity. Defence was clearly a motive for adding the sturdy west tower in the 12th century. With its thick walls and arrow slits, the resident priest was taking no chances in such insecure times.

Although stalwart and merciless in battle, Vikings maintained a deep faith in their sense of ultimate destiny and a belief in the afterlife. Proof of this came to light when a Viking sword and the precious Ormside Bowl were unearthed in the church graveyard.

Having survived intact for a millennium, this unique artefact was in remarkable condition. When first discovered in 1823 by a gravedigger, it was immediately recognised as a masterpiece of the Dark Ages and is now housed in York Museum for safety. Could this relic be the Luck of Ormside? Certainly, prosperity has seen fit to descend on this small community, even down to the splendid proportions of two arboreal celebrities (of which more anon). Perhaps W.G. Collingwood got it right when he suggested that the cup was a part of Orm's plunder and he 'gave it to the priest for the good of his soul' – Orm's that is!

Opposite the venerated mound lies Ormside Hall, dating from the 14th century, which supposedly has a secret passage connecting with the church. The entrance, however, has yet to be located. Once a thriving centre for the sale of cheese and butter, the market cross close to the hall was where business was conducted.

But during the Civil War the cross was destroyed, leaving only a circle of stone steps. Not until 1693 did the owner of Ormside Hall, Cyprian Hilton, decide to improve its amenity value by planting a sapling in the centre of the redundant central gap. Anyone who passes today will witness to what extent Hilton's sycamore has grown beyond all expectations to become the magnificent tree that now spreads its leafy tentacles across the bridleway.

Nurtured from a tiny seedling, the celebrated Cedar Tree at Little Ormside

The Walk

Continue past the tree to head south down the main street, forking left out of the village towards Ormside Mill. At a sharp right-hand corner just beyond the ford, pass through a gate to maintain a southerly direction alongside Helm Beck. Lean right to locate a gate and then continue across the next field towards a small copse.

Drop down left through the tree cover to find a clear path. Leave this when it veers right and cross a fence stile into an open field. Make your way to the far right corner and another fence stile. Then amble along the side of the railway to reach the road.

Cross the bridge to find a stile on the left pointing towards Heights Farm, three quarters of a mile to the south-west. Initially accompanying a hedge, the path passes through four gates before entering the farmyard to the left of the main house. Admire the new roof which, on my visit, was being erected in between showers by the farmer and his sons.

Beyond a gate at the far side, slant right past an old quarry to reach a back lane. Bear right for a quarter mile, then take the path on the left signposted to Catherine Holme. Keep left of a new planting of conifers before entering a fenced corridor. In contrast to regular hinged gates, this and the one at the far end are lift gates. A simple yet effective change as you will find.

Cross a footbridge to accompany a fenced stream on the left to the end of the field. Through a regular gate, the clear track then deposits us on Broadmire Road, opposite the entrance to Catherine Holme. Take a right past the Wesleyan chapel, where the week's cryptic message on my visit exhorted that we should, 'Better be a burden bearer than a burden maker'. What solicitation is offered to you?

Another 100 metres and a hidden stile on the left points the way west along a fenced plantation. Pass through a gate at the end and take a right

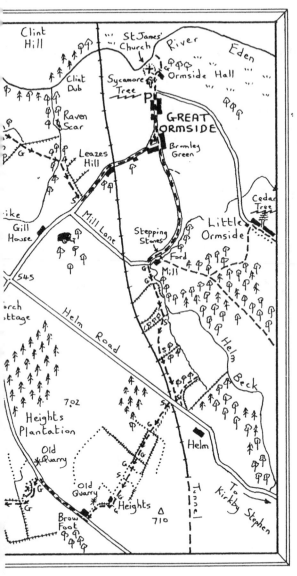

along an avenue of trees. Half way along this, a thin trod forks left across grassy pastures to cross the infant Hoff Beck by a substantial livestock bridge. Almost immediately thereafter, mount a fence stile on the right and make your way along the edge of a wood.

A pair of gates sandwiching a stile will bring you to the ford at Rutter Mill, which has been renovated for use as a café, offering welcome refreshment. Walk back upstream for 50 metres to observe Rutter Force at close quarters. In summer, a mere trickle, one can but imagine the hefty plunge of foaming spume as it pours over the lip in full flow.

Cross the road from the café to enter a field and continue along the left bank of Hoff Beck. Some 300 metres beyond the first stile, the right of way has been diverted over a footbridge to the far side. It then keeps to the raised river terrace past a cattle bridge to the next walkers' footbridge a mile downstream. Here we return to the west bank, continuing north through a gate and along a hedged passage into a back lane.

Bear right up to the B6260 and the hamlet of Hoff. Head towards Appleby to swing right over a stile immediately after crossing Hoff Beck by the road bridge. Make a diagonal furrow towards the tree-clad banking on the left, angling in to cross a fence stile. Then stick with the edge of Rowley Wood until Lookingflatt is reached.

The owners have kindly given permission for walkers to use their farm access track to reach Helm Road. Straight opposite, a gate enables continued progress along a hedge and minor rill originating from Tilekiln Ponds. Beyond the next fence stile you must negotiate an overgrown and rather marshy depression before emerging into an open field.

Bear half right aiming for a gate, and then continuing south-east to cross Gill Sike and its chaperone of trees. A further 200 metres will deposit you on the lane serving Great Ormside. Head left for the last half mile back to this primeval site.

Before leaving, take a drive up the narrow cul-de-sac linking the main village to its tiny offshoot. Outside Orm Lodge, another symbol of health and vigour soars up to shake hands with the pewter cloud base.

It was General Whitehead who nurtured a minute seedling in his hat whilst returning from Lebanon in the mid 19th century. Sharing his meagre water ration during the long voyage, the infant cedar survived to become the regal specimen that proudly graces the lodge's garden.

Walk 9

Keswick: The Druids' Circle

Mystery:	Castlerigg GR 291236
Distance:	4½ miles
Total Height Climbed:	300 feet (92 metres)
Nearest Centre:	Keswick
Start and Finish:	Park on the right of the A591, just beyond the right fork up Castle Lane.
Map:	Ordnance Survey English Lakes, 1:25 000, north-west area

Mystical and abstruse, the stone circles of Cumbria present a fascinating conundrum that still baffles all who seek to delve into their obscure past. Of the seventeen known circles, the most accessible and renowned is that located two miles east of Keswick at Castlerigg.

Thought to be of Neolithic origin, the stones are generally assumed to have a religious significance associated with the pagan rituals performed by Druid priests. Ancient relics have always attracted interest, pointing as they do to man's earliest colonisation of the region. And none more so than Castlerigg. Not the most haunting of locations, an honour reserved for the Swinside example, it nevertheless offers a prodigious insight into the primitive beliefs of Bronze Age man.

The Walk

Our route today avoids the crowds that are wont to visit the ancient site by exploring the lower reaches of the unfrequented Naddle Valley. Walk back towards the entrance serving High Nest and fork left up the paved access road. The right of way pours between the buildings of this old farmstead to pass through a gate, then continuing alongside a wall on the right.

Take note that many of the field boundaries hereabouts comprise an amalgam of drystone walling and ugly fencing. Beyond a small clutch of fenced conifers, mount a stile, after which the path forges ahead over grassy pastures to an offset wall. Go over a ladder stile and another is reached in 100 metres, as the Castlerigg enclosure is neared.

Direct access is not possible, the path funnelling into a narrow corridor with trees on the right. Pass through a gate into a back lane, where you take a left to gain the entrance to the revered site. Due to its ease of access, some restriction of movement within the perimeter of the site has been imposed in an attempt to prevent further erosion of the grassy concourse. It is hoped that re-seeding of the worst affected areas will help protect the monument for future generations.

One of the earliest visitors to record this experience was the poet Thomas Gray, whose *Journal in the Lakes* (1769) helped to stimulate an embryonic tourist industry. He counted fifty stones in total, the largest at over 2.5 metres in height, set in a ring 108 feet in diameter.

John Keats' lack of enthusiasm for the site was doubtless emboldened by the rain-lashed November day of his visit. The poet's sombre description of, 'A dismal cirque, Of Druid stones upon a forlorn moor'. was included in an epic sonnet called *Hyperion*.

With much of the Lakeland year dawning murky and grey, early rituals performed upon the windswept hillock must have appeared forbidding to a simple peasantry. Tiers of serrated rock pirouette in haughty disdain on all sides, casting a hypnotic allure that has continued to enchant visitors since the dawn of time.

Explanations as to the prime function of these strange henges continues to baffle even the most ardent scholar. In addition to religious associations, one theory suggests that many of the British stone circles were aligned to the movement of the sun, moon and stars, using a measurement referred to by Alexander Thom as the megalithic yard (2.72 feet). Certainly it has been shown that Castlerigg and Cross Fell in the Pennines are in line with Long Meg, which happens to coincide with the rising sun on 1 May.

Such a puzzling dilemma is likely to enhance all manner of intriguing allegories. One such concerns the practice of human sacrifices to appease the gods for continued prosperity of the community. In this particular instance it was a plague that had ravaged the village near to Castlerigg, wherein dwelt two lovers named Mudor and Ella.

Satisfaction for these recalcitrant gods could only be achieved through the sacrificial offering of a virgin by fire. Shouldering this heavy responsibility, the druid priests gathered inside the vestry of the circle to draw lots as to the fate of the luckless maiden. And you've guessed it. Ella was chosen.

She accepted her destiny as saviour of the tribe with a composure and sense of decorum that was indeed laudable. Mudor was, however, less than chivalrous when he learned the dreadful news. But no entreaty would sway the druid elders.

At the appointed hour, the sacrificial pyre beneath the mountain fastness was lit. As smoke billowed forth and the burning wood crackled, a rock behind the altar split asunder and a torrent of water gushed forth to douse the flames. Mudor's prayers had been answered. The young man

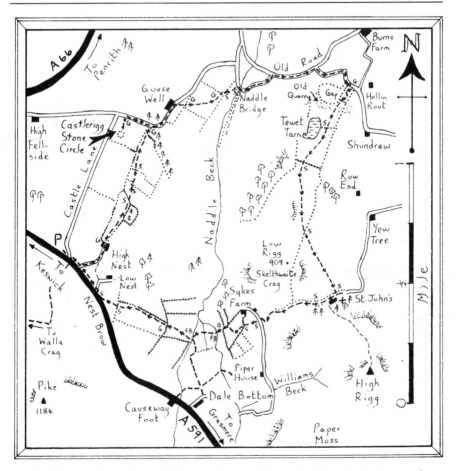

rushed forward to release his loved one, and from that time human sacrifice was no longer tolerated. Soon after the druid cult faded away, but the mysticism that surrounds the ancient relic still survives.

Dominating the area around Castelrigg is the most eye-catching colossus in Lakeland. Like some primordial beast of prey carousing over its unfortunate prey, Blencathra hovers with menacing arrogance above his domain. No fell wanderer can remain passive for long, nor resist the statuesque challenge flung out by his craggy skeleton. Keep him in mind for another expedition.

As with all esteemed predators, those who come to gaze and fawn upon Blencathra do so from a distance. And the most popular locale has to be Castlerigg. From here, the sinewy tautness of the muscular torso is revealed in all its nobility. Winter is the prime season for such voyeurs, when ice sparkling along the ridges brings out the contours to perfection. Crystal clear ozone emphasises the sublime beak as it pecks at the scudding bolls of cotton wool floating overhead.

Maybe the ambience that surrounds Castlerigg is complementary, the two being welded into a nebulous fusion that only serves to ensnare those who come to share in a mystery that only Lakeland could create. Nobody can deny that here lies the most favoured site of photographers wishing to capture the quintessential mien that depicts Blencathra, without straying too near the brooding presence.

Back on the road, head east around a bend towards Gosse Well, where the farm buildings have been converted into small workshops. Take the path opposite through a gate to cross a short field to the next gate. Aim diagonally down the grass slope for the far left corner. Beyond the gate, slant right to a wall stile and go across the brief sward to rejoin the back lane through a gate.

Take a right to cross Naddle Beck and so up the old road. Now superseded by the new A66 trunk road, this tortuous alternative gives some idea of the leisurely course that travellers once 'enjoyed'. A mixed blessing, the new road provides rapid transit to Keswick and West Cumbria whilst encouraging more visitors from further afield.

Turn down the first right, which gives access to the splendid rift of St John's-in-the-Vale. Watch for a gate on the right signposted to St John's Church. A zigzag track climbs this extreme northern shoulder known as Naddle Fell. Pass through a wall gap to gain the rolling terrain adjacent to Tewit Tarn.

Once over a wall stile on the left of the placid waters, mount the easy grass bank ahead. Beyond a fence stile, stroll across a shallow depression and up the facing slope of Low Rigg. A glance to the north-west will reveal Castlerigg surmounting an elongated knoll. From this elevated position, it becomes easier to place the ancient relic in its true context amid what used to be a wild and lonely place.

A wall crosses the fell, soon crossed by a stile on the gradual descent to the col between Low and High Riggs. Secreted within a sconce of conifers, the tiny church of St John is easily missed. The foremost building is the Carlisle Diocesan youth centre, which shelters beneath the louring crags above. Those with an abundance of vigour to spare might elect to have lunch atop the ridge proper. A clear path climbs the slope behind the centre to gain the summit of High Rigg.

Less energetic souls should head due west, passing through a gate and descending the broad cross-fell track linking the parallel valleys of St John's and Naddle. At the bottom, cross straight over the access road serving Sykes Farm to pass through a stile. Make a beeline over slabs of rock for the fence below. Mount the stile to cross the flat valley pasture but keep to the narrow grass causeway to avoid trampling the 'growing crop'.

Take a sharp right in the middle to reach the other side and then continue along to the far right corner. Pass through a gate and another 50 metres will bring you to a lean footbridge, gated at either end. This enables Naddle Beck to be negotiated. Ahead, the shattered bones of Goat Crag control the western flank of this brief tributary dale.

After tramping over the next field, a T-junction of tracks is reached. Fork right over a flat bridge to ascend the western slope. Pass through a gate to stick with the fence on your right up to the field corner. A stile can be located 10 metres to the left along the wall. Cross the next field aiming half right to gain the main road, then turn right towards Keswick for a further quarter mile.

Outstandingly evocative of man's primitive genesis, a visit to Castlerigg, and indeed others of its genre, will provoke an inquisition into the very core of our being. Here, then, is presented a hard copy of our ancient history that emphatically demands confrontation. The real question to be postulated concerns the progress of man himself during the interim.

Castlerigg Stone Circle

Walk 10
Caldbeck: D'ye Ken?

Mysteries:	John Peel's Grave GR 325399, the Branthwaite Dog GR 3037
Distance:	6 miles
Total Height Climbed:	450 feet (137 metres)
Nearest Centre:	Caldbeck
Start and Finish:	Park in the official car park in the village, which is located on the B5299, after crossing Cald Beck.
Map:	Ordnance Survey Pathfinder 576, Caldbeck

Crammed full of intriguing asides that belie its modest physical proportions, the village of Caldbeck nestles in a shallow trough on the extreme northern fringe of Lakeland. Although the industries that once brought prosperity have now declined in favour of tourism, the village still retains an independent spirit that manages to combine its rich heritage with a contemporary approach by building upon old traditions. Indeed, it boasts an active local community, even to the extent of having its own squash court.

Throughout the 18th century, wool and corn mills abounded, with one mill even producing paper, and there was also an all-important brewery. By 1829, prosperity was outwardly visible (and inwardly imbibed) in the form of six public houses. Today, only the Oddfellows Arms is left. Many of the old mills, once powered by the spluttering surge of the 'cold stream', have been transformed into other uses such as a brewery and mining museum.

Take time out to wander round the well-ordered settlement, giving special attention to the church of St Kentigern. Dedicated to the pioneering zeal of that crusading cleric St Mungo, of whom we will hear more on Walk 23, it is more renowned for the legendary huntsman who lies beneath the hallowed turf in the graveyard.

Although many people worked in the copper and lead mines of the Caldbeck Fells up until 1960, farming has always been a regular source of employment. But for John Peel, a farmer born and bred, a mythical reputation was earned through his fanaticism as a hunter. Running with the hounds became his sole abiding passion.

From dawn until the fox was eventually caught or escaped, he would rally his pack for the chase, after which a dram or two in one of the local hostelries was downed with 'spirit'. It was perhaps fitting that he met his final denouement in a hunting accident in 1854, at the grand age of 78 years.

He usually wore a heavy overcoat of 'Iveson Grey' which is referred to in the immortal ditty penned by his friend John Woodcock Graves. Unlike the rough and ready huntsman, Graves disliked Cumberland so much that he emigrated to Tasmania in 1833. Without doubt, it is this song more than anything else that made John Peel a household name.

I well remember as a young sprocket that it was a favourite in the school radio sing-a-long programmes, when we were all convinced that Peel's first name was Ken! For those unfortunate enough to have missed the opportunity to raise the roof which such legendary melodies, here is a brief taster. To be sung in ebullient fashion, preferably accompanied by a swinging tankard:

> *'D'ye ken John Peel with his coat so grey,*
> *D'ye ken John Peel at the break of day,*
> *D'ye Ken John Peel when he's far, far away*
> *With his hounds and his horn in the morning.'*

His decorated grave of white marble is easily found close to the church door. There is, however, another legendary character buried within St Kentigern's graveyard. The Beauty of Buttermere, Mary Robinson (See Walk 29), lies somewhere within its confines although I was unable to locate the site. Perhaps you will have more luck.

John Peel is buried in the graveyard

The Walk

Leave through the rear gate of the churchyard and cross Cald Beck. Turn left along Friars Row, a reminder that the first building was a hospice for travellers established by the Bishop of Carlisle in medieval times. Bear left opposite the car park to re-cross the beck on the B5299, slanting immediately right through the garden of the house on your left. Stiled at either end, it gives access to a meadow paralleling the beck. Pass through a gate at the far end to join a back lane.

Head right until a signpost points the way upstream between a pair of stone buildings. Stick with the path which veers towards the beck, where the old mill once turned out innumerable wooden bobbins for the textile industry. Gutted by a fire and never resurrected, the 42-foot water wheel that powered the mill was reckoned to be the largest in England.

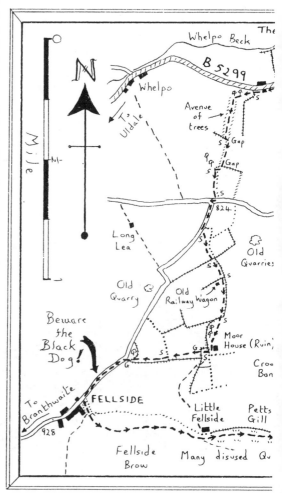

The path soon narrows into a rock stairway as it mounts the north bank of this impressive limestone gorge known as The Howk. Meaning 'great cave' or 'grotto', the name was first recorded in 1777, and serves to indicate that the fissure was at one time an underground cavern.

Enormous swallow holes abound in the pockmarked bed of the gorge. The largest, referred to as The Fairies' Kitchen, presents the illusion of boiling water when the fermenting cascade is in full spate. Approaching Fairy Bridge, thought to be the site of the original cavern roof, a continuously roaring, spume pummels the steep rock walls. Akin to the riotous fanfare of a satanic orchestra, it assaults the eardrums with unrestrained fury.

Cross the wooden bridge to

climb out into the field on the south bank above. Then accompany the fence around to join the B5299. Bear right past a cottage called Todcroft, where Mary Robinson spent her latter years in peace and obscurity with her second husband. Walk along the road for 300 metres until a stile on the left marks the start of a track across the fields.

Follow the grooved route with an intermittent tree-lined guard of honour which becomes more pronounced as the easy gradient is climbed. Pass through a gap, swapping to the left side of a hedge and so up to another, there to bear right along a wall. Cross a stile and continue south along this wall to reach a back lane.

Turn right for 50 metres and then left along the Fellside road. After 300 metres, mount a stile and take the footpath, maintaining a southerly course. Beyond the next stile, listen out for the 'singing gate'. This tubular steel construction blows a cool refrain when the wind deems to co-operate.

After negotiating two more stiles, pass left of a small, fenced copse to arrive at the abandoned farmstead of Moor House, now merely a ruin harking back to more prosperous times for the small farmer. Confined to larger and more accessible units, the industry struggles to compete with the bright lights and pay packets offered by the city.

Cross a wall stile soon passing through a gate. Head west alongside a fence to re-join the road through another gate. Bear left towards Fellside, keeping a wary eye open for the Branthwaite Dog known to frequent this section of highway. This phantom black hound has been seen charging along the road on numerous occasions. Mysteriously appearing as if from nowhere, and as quickly vanishing into thin air, it has haunted the area for generations.

Slant left along a walled track at the edge of the village, which was the home of one of Lakeland's most celebrated shepherds. Pearson Dalton, who spent his working life based at Skiddaw House, returned here at weekends. For forty-seven years, he tended sheep on the fells at the 'back o' Skidda' with only a battery powered radio and a few tattered books for company.

But Pearson enjoyed his hermit-like existence and saw no reason to retire. Sometimes cut off for weeks on end due to blizzards and snow drifts, age eventually caught up with the old recluse and he was compulsorily retired in 1969, going to live with his sister in Fellside.

Follow the track serving the isolated dwelling of Little Fellside. Keep above the intake wall past the farm, heading east across a marshy tract and staying parallel with a fence as far as Petts Gill. Go through a wall gate and then along a fence, turning left into the farmyard. Bear right along the access road and accompany it all the way to the settlement of Nether Row.

Circle left, heading north down the road for 200 metres until a clear track forks right. Walk along this for a half mile to cross straight over the metalled right of way serving Hudscales. Two stiles need to be climbed before entering a large field. Cross this, nudging a wall corner to arrive at a grassy lane leading down to Street Head.

Step over one stile and another on the left to follow a fence down to a road. Head left for 100 metres only, there to mount a stile on the opposite side. Stick with the wall up to a gate and cross the next field to its far left corner, keeping right of the farm buildings that comprise Matthew Rudding. A stile and a patch of rough land will deposit you in the farmyard.

Exit along the unmade access road in a general westerly direction, to the edge of Townhead. Mount a wall stile and follow a hedge north to a fence stile, after which the enclosed crossing of Gill Beck is made using a neat footbridge. A narrow pathway hemmed in by fence and hedge leads past new housing to the main road at the western limit of Caldbeck.

Here, William Strong carries on the traditional craft of clog making. The family business has been in the old, stone premises for over 50 years. His main line is the Derby Clog favoured by truck drivers and farmers. Their great advantage according to William is that they are good for your feet, hard wearing and warm in winter but cool in summer. Just one more of the traditional crafts that make Caldbeck a true reminder of a Lakeland that has largely disappeared.

Walk 11

Appleby: Infamy at Gaythorne Hall

Mystery:	The Hairy Man's Hole GR 650133
Distance:	6 miles
Total Height Climbed:	500 feet (152 metres)
Nearest Centre:	Great Asby
Start and Finish:	Drybeck has limited parking space along the roadside close to Town Head Farm.
Map:	Ordnance Survey Pathfinder 597, Crosby Ravensworth and Brough

Lying but a mile east of the Tebay to Appleby road, the secluded valley of Scale Beck offers a rare charm characteristic of rural Westmorland. Although the initial section of this walk lies along the celebrated Westmorland Way connecting Appleby and Arnside, I met no other walkers here or on the rest of the circuit.

Remote and unassuming, this delectable corner of the old county guarantees that degree of contentment enjoyed by those who favour their own company. Cast your eye over the undulating vista with not another soul in sight. Verdant pastures roll away unhindered until the backbone of the Pennine Chain swallows them up.

Much of the land hereabouts forms part of the Levens estate and is owned by the Bagot family. Focusing on Gaythorne Hall, investigation of the singular if grim event that occurred in this bleak Elizabethan farmstead will follow in due course.

The Walk

But first we must take a walk up the metalled lane signposted to Gaythorne Hall at the western limit of Drybeck hamlet. Motorists who assume this to be a short cut to the hall will be sadly disillusioned when the road terminates at a gate. In actuality, the road provides access to the isolated buildings of The Wraes and Highfield.

Arrow-straight, the lane ends after a mile, when we pass through the gate marking the start of the bridleway. Crossing an open field, the track heads south-west past Heading's Wood on the right. At the end of the trees lies another gate. Beyond this, the walled track soon opens out, which is where we branch left down a stony farm track serving Gaythorne Hall.

After swinging to the right, the path crosses Scale Beck and goes up a walled section to the hall itself. Grey, stone walls several feet thick provide extensive accommodation for the Lord family who run this Levens outpost of about 1000 acres. Below ground level are numerous rooms which once housed more than just cattle.

One of these brought a certain notoriety to Gaythorne in the early years of the 19th century and has become known as The Hairy Man's Hole. It concerns a mixed marriage, which in those days referred to Protestant and Catholic as against the racial connotations in today's parlance. Unable to decide in what faith their child was to raised, they locked him in a dingy cellar with only a tiny window for air and light.

Fed through a hole in the door, the poor child grew up in filth and squalor like a wild animal. This bizarre incarceration finally ended when a huntsman caught sight of a hairy arm waving from the small window. Only capable of uttering harsh grunts, his back covered in hair, the youngster was taken to Appleby. There he became a respectable citizen of some substance, even attaining the office of mayor.

Sceptics claim that the story was invented to incite religious disquiet among the populace. Certainly, like many such legends, the facts have become a little blurred with age. The mother of the current owner of Levens has, however, intimated that her great grandmother actually met the man in question,

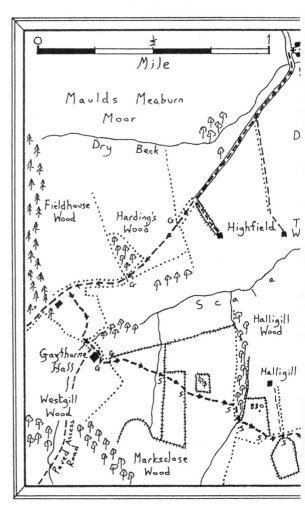

who verified the nature of his strange upbringing.

A gate gives entry to the farmyard abutting the hall, its thick walls concealing a grim history. Bear left down a short passage and through a gate at the end into the field beyond. Accompany a fence on the left for 100 metres before cutting up a grassy rise by a prominent post. Maintain a south-easterly bearing across the low knoll, aiming for a fence stile that soon appears over the lip.

Another parallel fence stile follows in quick succession. Thereafter, skirt the upper edge of an enclosed planting of trees, making for the right of Halligill Wood. Climb a wall stile and lean immediately right alongside the wall to cross a small tributary stream feeding into Scale Beck.

Continue across the next field to a stile in the wall, after which a left wheel will bring you to another fence stile. Here, the right of way has been paved to give easy access to Halligill. Follow it all the way down to where it merges with another serving Whitewall.

After a further 100 metres, at the far side of a cattle grid, the road veers sharply to the right. Follow the wall on your left around to a stile. Pathless at this point, our route makes a wide right-hand loop in a dry valley to pass through a wall gate.

Slant up to the far left corner of the field, where a stile will be located tucked beneath a leafy bough. At the far side of a grassy lane serving a barn, pass through a gate and progress up the right side of a long, narrow field. At its far end, mount a wall stile which deposits you in an enclosed field access track.

Bear right and follow the well-hooved trod to another stile. The path then becomes more solid underfoot, continuing ahead with only a fence on the left before striking right along the bottom edge and up to a gate. From here, it swings left, keeping close to a hedge through another gate and down to the access track serving a cottage known as Scale Beck.

Any strange screeching noises that might crack the peaceful mood are likely to emanate from the family peacock. Concealed from casual observation, this 17th-century, whitewashed cottage is, indeed, what every townie dreams about when stuck in a traffic jam in downtown Oswaldtwistle. Take a right after the gate along the track to arrive at a back lane.

Bear left for less than a mile back to Drybeck. Crossing the watercourse from which the hamlet derives its name, one can see that upstream from the bridge it rapidly disappears into a jungle of vegetation. Turn left after crossing the bridge to walk the length of this sleepy enclave back to the starting point.

Gaythorne Hall

Walk 12

Askham: The Grim Reaper Pays a Call

Mysteries:	Elizabeth Kirkbride of Askham, Moor Divock
Distance:	6 miles
Total Height Climbed:	550 feet (168 metres)
Nearest Centre:	Askham
Start and Finish:	Park along the elongated main street of Askham, on either side of the village green, but please avoid parking on the grass.
Map:	Ordnance Survey English Lakes, 1:25 000, north-east area

From Land's End to John O' Groats, eyes sparkle with interest when charismatic names such as Wasdale and Great Langdale are mentioned. Haweswater is also likely to elicit suitable nods of recognition as a principle source of Corporation Pop for the Manchester conurbation. Few will have any inkling that this major reservoir drains into the River Lowther.

Meandering down a valley that has always been overshadowed by its more illustrious colleagues, the river has its origins amid the circlet of fells around the tiny reservoir of Wet Sleddale. In parallel with the eastern boundary of the Lake District National Park, here is a domain remote from familiar trails, where little has changed over centuries.

Much of the valley forms part of the Lowther estate, home to a prestigious family that ruled these northern tracts with an iron fist for many a long year. The name of Lowther was both feared and respected throughout Cumbria for a substantial part of the present millennium. Now more renowned for its wildlife adventure park, the crennelated battlements of the old castle poke above the switch of coniferous trees, commanding attention when viewed from the fells above Askham. Now merely a ruined shell, it harks back to an age of extravagant pageantry.

Villages named from the Old English derivation including Helton, Bampton and Askham indicate that the valley remained undiscovered by the Norse invaders whose place names dominate Lakeland. Or maybe their attempts at settlement and mastery of the local populace were vigorously repulsed. Suffice to say that the Lowther Valley epitomises a tradition that is more English than fish and chips or Jennings Bitter, and equally as appealing.

Yet the tranquil calm that permeates the atmosphere was not always so refreshing. In the latter part of the 19th century, death stamped its indelible mark on the villages of Helton and Askham, sending a chilled ripple of trepidation into the hearts of the rustic inhabitants. Neither before nor since has the Grim Reaper swept through this tiny enclave with such devastating and tragic consequences. The macabre circumstance unfolded in Liverpool, where Elizabeth Kirkbride lived with her husband and four children until his death in 1864.

Returning to Helton, she left her children in the charge of their grandmother in Askham, presumably due to lack of space. Or was it for some more sinister purpose? As time passed one of the children paid a visit to his mother, only to discover the mummified body of a baby in the attic. On returning to Askham, the boy was sworn to secrecy by his grandmother, doubtless to avoid shaming the family name.

On a further surreptitious visit he unearthed another dead body in the garden. And still he remained silent. It was to be a further seven years before the full horror finally emerged in all its gruesome reality. Four tiny bodies, one having a cord tightly pulled round its neck, were uncovered in the luggage of Elizabeth Kirkbride, who had been traced to a lodging house in Liverpool.

Stone circle on Moor Divock

At this point the police were summoned and the lady in question arrested. Unable to prove the charge of murder, she was found guilty only of concealing the deaths of her children and served a little over two years in prison.

It later transpired that a 'respected' local tradesman had fathered the children, probably conspiring with Elizabeth to conceal their bizarre liaison in such a horrific manner. Although he never admitted the affair, the cad was thereafter shunned by the local citizenry of this tightly-knit community and his business collapsed. Both he and Elizabeth disappeared into obscurity and nobody heard from them again. Whether he continued the scurrilous affair with his mistress has never been established.

Consider these facts whilst walking up Askham's main street, which exhibits an old world charm, spread out on either side of the village green. A linear settlement at right angles to the valley road which slices it in half, the cottages on the left possess long, narrow plots at the rear, in keeping with early strip farming practices.

The Walk

Continue uphill out of Askham towards Moor Divock, until the access road serving Whitbysteads veers sharply to the left. Maintain a direct course with the wall on your right, heading south-west past a patch of gorse. Ignore a track branching left into Mirebank Plantation as the final intake wall is neared.

Pass through a gate to emerge on Riggingleys Top, overlooking the wild, upland plateau of Moor Divock. Stands of bracken and tough moorland grass interspersed with shake holes stretch away towards the high fells. A clear, grassy corridor forges a passage though the initial bracken, indicating the direction to be taken.

After a slight descent, follow this route to the south-west for a half mile until the principal cross-fell route linking Pooley Bridge with the Lowther Valley is reached. Swing left along the wide, level concourse which has crossed this desolate wilderness since time immemorial. More than any other locality, Moor Divock abounds in primeval antiquities that still continue to attract archaeologists and historians intent on resurrecting more of our past culture.

An ancient stone circle is soon passed on the left, followed a short time later by the unequivocal Cop Stone. Fork left of this along a thin trod that crosses the open fell road after 300 metres. Drop down to the limestone wall encircling the moor and cross it by a ladder stile. Pick a diagonal course over the field to the far left corner and through a gate accompanying the next wall down to another gate.

Take note of the strip terracing that is still visible centuries after this type of feudal farming was abandoned. Enter a walled pathway for only 50 metres, until a stile on the left points the way across the adjoining field. Aim for the far left corner and a stile hidden by the hedge. Then stick with the wall on your left to another stile at the end.

Cross the next field to the boundary wall's halfway point and go over a stile, continuing diagonally down to reach the back lane at the edge of Helton where Elizabeth Kirkbride met with her lover. No more than 50 metres to the left a track breaks right to link with the main valley road that bypasses the village.

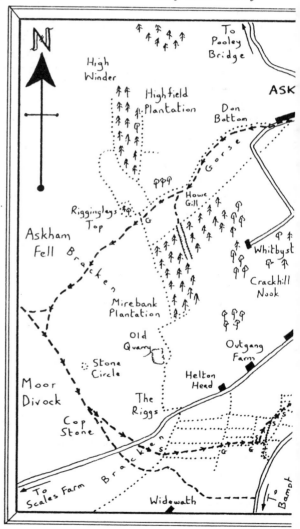

Continue straight across and over a stile, where access is provided to a narrow passage with a gate at valley level. Slant across the field to meet with the River Lowther at a substantial footbridge gated at either end.

At the far side, bear right to mount a stile and then follow the fence left up to the road cutting along the east side of the valley. Go straight across and up the access road serving the small hamlet of Whale, a principal settlement hereabouts prior to the common land being enclosed into the field system that characterises today's countryside.

Beyond the first cottage on the left, take the signposted footpath along an enclosed passageway abutting the garden. The path is stiled at each end. Emerging into one of the common grazing fields that have escaped wholesale enclosure, slant half right past Whale

Farm. Aim for a stile part way along the fence to enter the enclosed coniferous woodland.

Once in the wood, stick with the boundary fence to its far end, passing through a gate and maintaining a direct line to another gate close to a bend in the river. Accompany the fenced woodland that lines the river bank on your left across Low Deer Park.

The Lowther Valley is of particular geological significance – separating as it does the Borrowdale Volcanic rocks from the Carboniferous Limestone scars which form a distinctive rim along the upper edge of the valley.

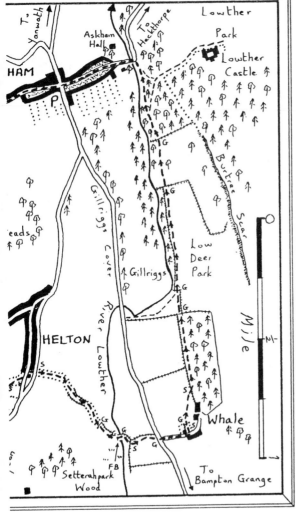

Beyond the next gate the track rises slightly to enter the gloomy forest by another gate. Keep to the lower path through the heavy tree cover as it drops down to follow the river bank. Arriving at Askham Bridge, cross to the far side and ascend the road back to the village proper.

On the left is the church built by Robert Smirke in 1832, a quarter century after his more celebrated design of the castle, now merely a Gothic memorial. Higher up on the right is Askham Hall where current members of the family now reside.

Think well on the tragic events that took place along this placid reach of the River Lowther, and the rigid code of Victorian morality that drove a young mother to take such desperate action to conceal her shameful conduct.

Walk 13

Cockermouth: Deadly Haunts

Mysteries:	Tallentire Hall GR 104352, Green Bank GR 110355
Distance:	6½ miles
Total Height Climbed:	450 feet (137 metres)
Nearest Centre:	Tallentire
Start and Finish:	Park on a piece of rough ground at the north-east edge of Tallentire, at the Y-junction.
Map:	Ordnance Survey Pathfinder 575, Cockermouth and Maryport

Few visitors who penetrate the undulating pastoral surroundings beyond Lakeland's northern border will have chanced across the village of Tallentire. A tiny settlement secreted within a rolling trough of greenery, even its sole chapel has been de-commissioned into a family residence.

Outwardly displaying an air of calm detachment, the village harbours not one, but two secrets of sinister import. At either end of the village, the houses in question have witnessed dire episodes in their histories that are like to trigger a rippling spasm of trepidation down the spine. At Tallentire Hall, ensconced within verdant parkland, a young girl was murdered at some time in the distant past. Her headless corpse is said to walk the dark corridors, appearing at the window where the foul deed was perpetrated.

Below the window in question, a red fungus has spread along the ground and is known as 'the ghost's blood'. And no matter how often it is scrubbed clean, the growth keeps returning. Reckoned to be the bacteria Seratia marcescens, it has been used as a marking agent in bacteriological experiments. As the hall stands in private grounds, it is difficult to ascertain the veracity of the story. But think well on it as you battle up the village street towards the house known as Green Bank.

Clearly in view for all to see at the far end of the street, clad in a bright shade of green, the house was once used to store dead bodies following a local disaster, possibly resulting from a roof collapse at one of the numerous quarries in the vicinity. A teenager sleeping in a downstairs room awoke during the night to find her bed being vehemently shaken by some unseen force in 1951. Rapidly exiting the room, her fearful experience confirmed to locals that the house was haunted by spirits of the long deceased tenants.

Tallentire Hall

The Walk

After resisting the devilish enticements on offer, take the right fork out of the village heading east towards Tallentire Hill. At the crossroads, cross over and continue up the hedged track, passing the trig column in a field on the right.

Arrow-straight, the rough lane terminates at a gate. Beyond this, slant half left to the far corner of the field. Go through another gate and carry on alongside the wall, passing through two gates before entering the farmyard of Grange Grassings.

It is readily apparent from the most recent Ordnance Survey map that much of the grass pasture has been transformed into long, narrow fingers of coniferous plantings in this part of North Lakeland. Beyond the farm buildings, proceed along the access road for 100 metres, then lean right through a gated gap in the tree line. Follow the fence, heading north-east. What appears initially to be an alien craft from some distant galaxy perched on the knoll in front is merely a pop art radio beacon.

At the end of the field, open a gate and accompany the edge of dense conifers past a reedy tarn. Make a sharp left along the fence to an exit gate. Stick with the fence down through a gate to join the access track serving Eweclose. Wander down this southern flank of the shallow valley occupied

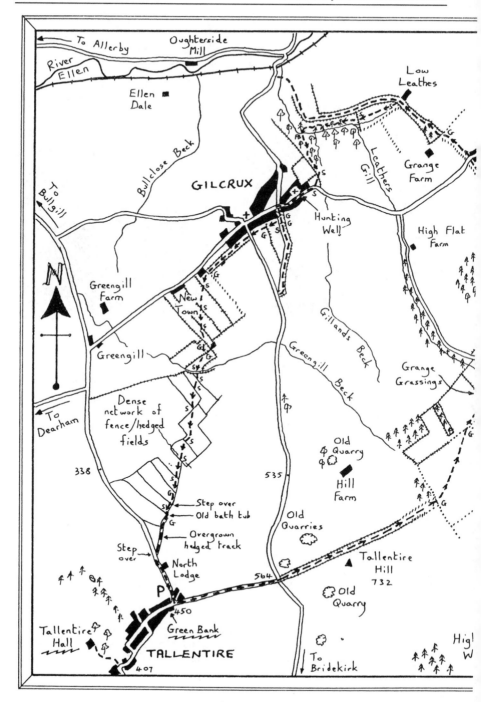

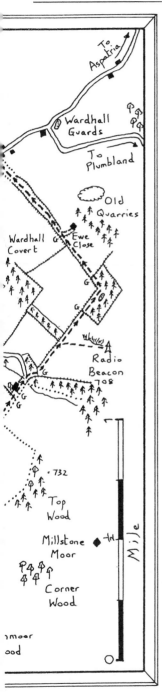

by the River Ellen to meet the Gilcrux road. The right of way continues on the far side, offset to the right. Keep with this track, passing Grange Farm on the left, and then go through a gate adjacent to another new plantation.

After passing left of Low Leathes, watch for a stile on the left which points the way along the upper edge of a tributary cutting of Leathers Gill. After crossing the grass pasture, mount a stile to enter an enclosed clutch of woodland. Meandering between the trees, the thin path soon arrives at an arch of naked firs. Like a railway tunnel, the far end appears as a lighted beacon, after which the path drops down to cross the footbridge over Leathers Gill.

Climb out of the leafy glade by means of a series of steps to the edge of the wood, thereafter accompanying the fence along a redirected path to a stile at the far end. Cross a piece of open ground to another stile giving on to the road at the eastern limit of Gilcrux.

Amble down the village street to the 14th-century church of St Mary, wherein a haglioscope in the chancel arch allows offset worshippers to follow the full service. Outside you will find the railed Hunting Well. Continue down past the old schoolhouse, keeping an eye open for the start of the right of way on the left just beyond the T-junction.

This route passes through a farmyard, along an old grassy lane and through two gates. Immediately after the second gate, bear right over a wall stile to walk along the rear edge of the back gardens, then through a gate to reach a back lane. Cross straight over and continue along a fenced track which terminates at a gate.

This gives onto the dense network of fenced/hedged fields stretching south from Gilcrux. Make a diagonal crossing of the next four fields, over stiles and heading in a general southerly direction. Aim for the corner of the fourth, adjoining a dilapidated structure. Pass through a gate cutting off the corner of the next field and continue to another gate.

Slant right to the far side of this field to stride over Greengill Beck and a fence stile on its opposite bank.

Slice off the corner of this field to step another stile. The next three fields follow a similar pattern, but the last needs sharp eyes to locate the hidden stile round the corner, where the field boundary has been removed. Crossing yet another field will bring you to a narrow but deep cutting alongside the fence.

Beyond this, accompany the fence on your left, first over a broken stile, then, soon after, a gate. This final section of the right of way between Gilcrux and Tallentire has been abandoned, with no effort to maintain it for the rightful passage of ramblers. From here on you are pioneering a long defunct track.

The next hedge has no stile but is easy to negotiate by using the numerous gaps and stepping over the single barbed wire strand. Further along on the left is what appears to be a stile over an old bath tub placed at the field corner for the benefit of the resident bovines. Whether for drinking or bathing is not made clear.

A gate now provides access to an overgrown, hedged lane complete with stream coursing down its midriff. Straddle as best you can for 100 metres until it veers away to the right. The final 200 metres terminates at a metalled highway where a strip steel fence must be crossed. Bear left down the road back to Tallentire.

Walk 14

Kirkby Stephen: Betwixt Two Castles

Mysteries:	Pendragon GR 782026, Lammerside GR 773048
Distance:	6 miles
Total Height Climbed:	650 feet (200 metres)
Nearest Centre:	Kirkby Stephen
Start and Finish:	Ample space is available for parking at the junction of Tommy Road and the B6259, opposite the gated entrance to Pendragon Castle.
Map:	Ordnance Survey Pathfinder 607, Tebay & Kirkby Stephen

Always a fascinating source of mystery and conjecture, castles have long fired the imaginations of all who chance upon them. Exploring these ancient moss-clad bones conjures up a host of bizarre perceptions equated with conflict and mayhem. None more so than Pendragon.

Secluded within the timeless beauty of the Upper Eden, this tree-girt edifice is easy to pass unawares. Harking back to an age when dark forces ranged the land, the low knoll on which the ruined castle stands was believed to harbour a legendary beast which struck fear into the simple peasantry who occupied the valley. Such a story led to the assumption that Uther Pendragon, father of King Arthur, built the original castle on what might well have been a Roman lookout post.

Never regarded as a benevolent chieftain, Uther is said to have ruled with an iron fist, despatching the Saxon hoards with ruthless abandon. To protect his home, the mighty warlord gave much thought to the problem of encircling his castle with a moat. A ditch excavated to contain the diverted waters can still be made out, even though the task was never completed. Hence the origin of the prophetic lines:

> *'Let Uther Pendragon do what he can*
> *Eden will run where Eden ran.'*

Like many powerful rulers, he was only brought to book by the scheming treachery of those unable to best him on the field of battle. In the year 515, all the inhabitants of Pendragon Castle, said to number over one hundred, died from poisoned water. Yet even in death, Uther's truculent spirit could

Pendeagon Castle – home to the father of King Arthur

not find peace. Often he has been seen on dark winter's nights, galloping at speed across the bleak expanse of Shap Fells on a snorting charger.

The ravages of time and neglect exacted a fearsome toll on Pendragon, which fell into disrepair over the next five centuries. It was to be the Clifford family who restored Pendragon to its former glory. Lady Anne in particular made diligent efforts to resurrect the fortunes of this once proud structure. Thus in 1661 she was at last able to spend time in the castle, even though her baggage train had to include a glazed window to exclude the draught from her bed chamber. Following her death in 1676, the castle once again fell into disrepair until its acquisition by the present owner, Raven Frankland, who has begun the delicate process of excavating the ancient monument. Explore with due care and respect these gutted remnants, which offer a tantalising glimpse into the violent drama played out beneath the sullen gritstone edges that characterise Mallerstang.

The Walk

Walk up Tommy Road, over Castle Bridge and the River Eden to swing sharp right at Low Cocklake. When the road veers left on to the open fell, continue ahead along a rough yet clear track heading north down the valley. On the left, a well-constructed lime kiln bears witness to the impor-

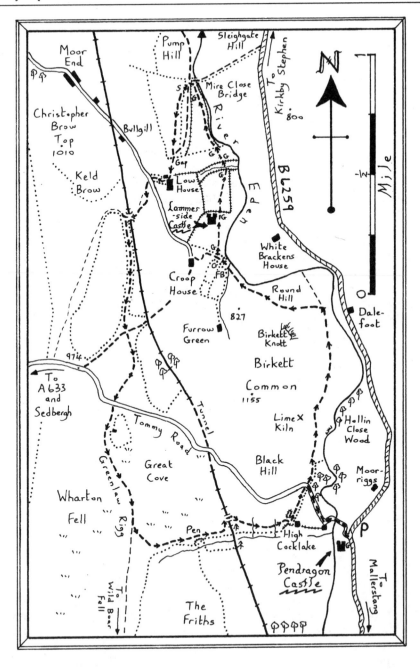

tance of this vital stone in the local economy. Follow the course of the Eden, maintaining a northerly direction for a further half mile until a severe left hander breaks from the onward trail down to the flood plain.

Circle around the base of Birkett Knott, where exposed ribs of grey, weathered rock puncture the verdant torso. The track passes left of Round Hill to once again parallel the river, and crosses a minor stream by a small footbridge. Soon, open a gate, and immediately pass through another on the right as you leave the main track.

Lammerside Castle stands alone and neglected in the middle of the grassy pasture, its gaunt façade crumbling and overgrown with vegetation. Only the local woollies now take shelter here, except of course for the ghosts of its mysterious past occupants. Smaller than Pendragon, Lammerside was built in the 13th century to protect the inhabitants from the ravages of marauding Scots invaders. It has, however, passed into Arthurian legend as the fabled Castle Dolorous, and home to a giant Saxon warrior named Tarquin who supposedly sated his hunger by eating young boys.

A further connection with Pendragon in the form of an underground connecting passage must, indeed, have its origins in pure fantasy. The only tunnel of any consequence hereabouts is that allowing passage of the Settle-Carlisle railway under Birkett Common.

It is believed that a certain Lambert must have been the first occupier, hence the name Lambert's Seat. What is known for certain about this singular abode is that the Whartons lived here prior to building their celebrated hall one mile to the north. Most of the stones were removed in the late 18th century to create field boundaries after the enclosure movement swept through the English countryside.

Beyond Lammerside, pass through a fenced gate and aim towards the far right corner of the next field. Two fenced gates in close proximity, followed soon after by one abutting a wall enable onward progress to be made. Keep a fence on your right as you follow the Eden downstream to Mire Close Bridge.

Beyond a gate, cross the access track serving Low House to slant half left where a stepped wall stile can be located. Accompany the wall on your left along a grassy shelf to merge with the gravel track close to a cattle grid. Stroll up to Low House and bear right past the farmhouse up a paved link road.

Cross over this back lane, which terminates at Croop House, and follow a rough track up to and across the railway by a stone bridge. Beyond a gate at the far side, turn sharp left along a broad, walled concourse for 200 metres. The track then veers right away from the railway, eventually passing beyond the intake walls into open country.

Slope in to join the rising wall on your left after crossing the main path to

Croop House. When the wall slants away to the left, continue ahead to cross Tommy Road and so up on to Greenlaw Rigg. This broad shoulder of moorland wilderness marks the northern extremity of Wild Boar Fell.

After passing the walled enclosure on your left, mount the gently rising swell of rough pasture making use of a rutted fell track. A further quarter mile should see you forking left off the track to meet the high intake wall, which can be followed down easy slopes to the railway.

The right of way crosses via a substantial stone bridge clearly provided for the highland pasturage. Continue down the hill to High Cocklake where the access road heads left, back to Tommy Road. Take a right down the road, retracing your steps to Pendragon at valley level.

Little has changed in this remote outpost of the upper Eden Valley since time immemorial, and I heartily recommend this historic walk on which you are unlikely to meet anyone. One can positively feel the spiritual presence of long departed warriors, tethered forever within the confines of their gaunt citadels.

Walk 15

Mungrisdale: Guardian of Mungrisdale

Mystery:	The Ghost Army GR 353289
Distance:	5 miles
Total Height Climbed:	950 feet (290 metres)
Nearest Centre:	Mungrisdale
Start and Finish:	Park on the grass verge alongside the swirling waters of the River Glenderamackin, opposite the village hall. Parking contribution requested.
Map:	Ordnance Survey English Lakes, 1:25 000, north-east area

Being an extension of the north-easterly tentacle stealing out from Blencathra's sinewy torso, Souther Fell is completely overshadowed by its more illustrious cousin. All eyes are inevitably drawn to the mesmerising ridge system splaying out in strident abandon. Yet this somewhat innocuous fell has achieved a measure of distinction in its own right that far outweighs that of its neighbouring Goliath.

An incident occurred along the domed ridge of Souther Fell some 250 years ago that was witnessed and attested by a legal attorney as an authentic verification that the incident was no idle fantasy. The Ghost Army of Souther Fell marched into the annals of Cumbrian history at a period when the Jacobite Rebellion of 1745 was getting under way.

Initially witnessed by a certain William Lancaster on Midsummer's Eve in 1735, he claimed to have seen a continuous flow of men and carriages perambulating across the top of the fell for more than an hour, until darkness fell blocking them from view. Not wishing to be ridiculed, he kept quiet about the incident until two years later when the very same thing happened again. On this occasion he brought his entire family out to support the visitation so none could dispute it.

Most notable, however, was the sighting in 1745 by twenty six locals of a formidable retinue of armed men and their baggage train straggling the length of the fell top. So affected were some witnesses that the next day they climbed the fell with the expectation of finding a vestige of such passage. But not a single footprint or wagon rut was to be seen.

And what of Daniel Strickland's experience whilst walking along the broad ridge later in 1774? Ahead he saw a troop of cavalry in uniform who immediately rode up a precipitous gradient impossible for normal horses to have negotiated. Only when he learned of the previous sightings was the faith in his sanity restored. No other spectral event received greater credence from contemporaries, which makes these circumstances all the more fascinating.

Certainly something was observed. Sceptics have suggested that it was a form of optical illusion, a mirage depicting the real Jacobite army on manoeuvres along the Scottish border to the north. Perhaps this is true as no further sightings have since been reported. But that fails to explain away the earlier account, and the observance of Daniel Strickland.

Souther Fell ridge, on the route of the ghost army

The only travellers likely to be seen these days will be those heading away from Souther Fell rather than on it, or the distant specks hurrying to gain a foothold on the ice-ravaged crags of Blencathra. Lonely and forlorn, you are more than likely to have the fell to yourself. All the better to consider the legendary ghost army which adds a splash of colour to a prosaic hummock that would otherwise have been of little significance.

One unusual feature of the fell that further sets it apart concerns its geographical situation. Virtually surrounded by the meandering flow of the Glenderamackin, it is denied island status only by the shallow depression known as Musthwaite Col. Beginning as a mere trickle, the river is forced around the whale-backed hump by way of Mungrisdale, effectively giving Souther Fell the standing of a peninsula.

The Walk

After parking in Mungrisdale, cross the tumbling waters of the Glendera-mackin by a footbridge to gain the back lane close to the Mill Inn. Once a traditional focal point for the local shepherds' meet, these gatherings were as much an excuse for a celebration as an exchange of errant woollies.

Avoid the temptation at this early stage to emulate those enduring characters by turning left along the back lane. After a quarter mile, pass through a gate and continue ahead for another 200 metres. Watch for a distinct track cutting back on the right of this bracken-cloaked, steep east face of Souther Fell. This was the route up which early Victorian tourists began their ascent of Blencathra from their base in Mungrisdale.

The route soon wheels sharply to the left, slanting up the rising bank through an initial swathe of bracken. It climbs steadily, following an obvious grass shelf until a clump of reeds precludes further onward progress. Here it is necessary to strike up the grass slope in a wide right-hand arc to attain the small summit cairn topping the fell.

Being the most easterly of the fells at the back o' Skidda has assured Souther Fell of an impressive panorama along the elongated backbone of England's premier mountain chain. But nobody would deny that the view is dominated by Blencathra's awesome profile, with the saddleback a prominent feature.

From the highest point, head south-west across the rolling sea of grass in the wake of the legendary army. Framed between the pitched outliers of Clough Head and Blencathra, the rugged skyline is controlled by the centrefold, which is none other than Scafell Pike.

Heed well this haunting epistle from the pen of Wordsworth as you proceed:

> *'Silent the visionary warriors go,*
> *Wending in ordered pomp their upward way,*
> *Till the last banner of the long array*
> *Had disappeared, and every trace is fled*
> *Of splendour – save the beacon's spiry head,*
> *Tipt with eve's latest gleam of burning red.'*

After crossing a shallow depression, fork right along a thin trail to visit a less poetic promontory mounted on the rim overlooking the valley of the Glenderamackin. Across the deep rift, Bannerdale Crags soar aloft, hemming in this meandering river.

Regain the main ridge path to descend the gently shelving sward to Mousthwaite Col. On either side, the alternating flow of the river clearly illustrates the anomaly of Souther Fell's geography, unique in Lakeland.

Locate a thin path slanting down to cross the river, and so join the route

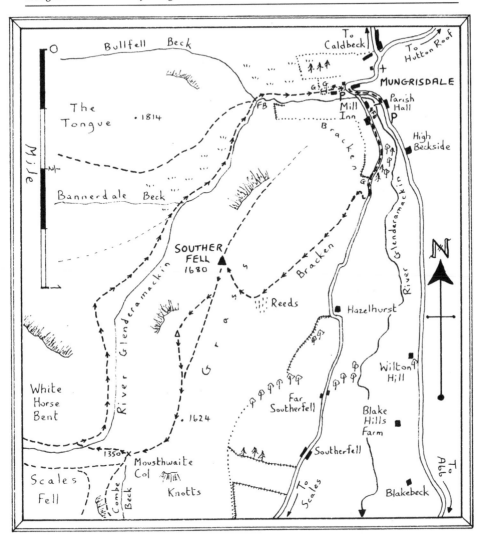

down valley which skirts around White Horse Bent. Descending from Mungrisdale Col, the track soon veers north on a parallel course to the Glenderamackin. Thereafter, it swings away before closing in again at the entrance to Bannerdale. Cross the beck issuing from this deep tributary valley, noting the honed circlet of louring teeth at its helm.

Accompanying the left bank of the river across the flat valley bottom, our route swings to the right on the approach to Mungrisdale village. The track homes into the intake walls to pass through a pair of gates into a walled corridor providing access to the open fell country. Turn right down the main street, returning to the village hall. Or walk up the back lane if some liquid refreshment is sought at the Mill Inn, whilst reflecting on Souther Fell's unusual claim to immortality.

In his *The History of Cumberland* (1793), William Hutchinson offers a detailed account of the spectral army which is hard to denigrate. And who would wish to. When a dank pall of grey mist hangs over the fell, and the wind hums a mournful dirge through the swaying tussocks of grass, all manner of bizarre speculations can invade the human mind.

Walk 16

Grange-in-Borrowdale: Into the Jaws

Mystery:	The Professor of Adventure GR 251160
Distance:	7 miles
Total Height Climbed:	850 feet (260 metres)
Nearest Centre:	Grange
Start and Finish:	Turn right off the B5289 to cross the double bridge spanning the River Derwent. Park on the piece of open ground on the right prior to entering the village proper.
Map:	Ordnance Survey English Lakes, 1:25 000, north-west area

Even the stoutest heart is apt to quake with trepidation as the snapping 'Jaws of Borrowdale' are approached. Here, road and river squeeze through the narrow gap pinched on either hand by the volcanic elbows of Kings How and Castle Crag. From earliest times generations of settlers have recognised the strategic value of the Jaws by establishing a stronghold atop Castle Crag's knobbly pate. No invader could possibly sidle past without boulders and other life-threatening apparatus being hurled from above.

It remains one of the few such hill forts that can positively be dated. And the impregnable site must have been occupied in Roman times if the artefacts unearthed amidst the scree-choked slopes are anything to go by. Indeed, the name Borrowdale itself stems from the Norse 'borgar dalr', which translates as 'valley of the fortress'.

But once the valley had settled into a peaceful haven, it was the solid composition of the Crag that attracted attention. Today, the sturdy cone is pockmarked with quarry detritus which must be negotiated if the summit ramparts are to be conquered. A stiff haul up from the old road, the ascent is worthy of much loftier acclaim than its measured height will allow.

Visitors motoring down Borrowdale from the direction of Keswick for the first time might well cast a wary eye to the craggy upsurge that greets them beyond Grange. In the 18th century the poet Thomas Gray refused to advance further, claiming that 'the crags now begin to impend terribly over your way'.

His exaggerated phraseology ensured that for most early tourists the Bowder Stone was to be the limit of their adventures. Yet by remaining in

Grange, Gray was able to produce one of the most colourful renditions of the Lakeland scene in his immortal *Journal*.

Another correspondent who was equally verbose described the view that confronted him in 1769 as being composed of 'beauty, horror and immensity united'. Dr John Brown's lyricism might well appear quaint and a trifle absurd in an age of new technology, but such reports, emphasising the scourge of naked cliffs, transfixed visitors, who were in awe of the majestic setting.

The fear and alarm inspired by this fearsome place was doubtless stimulated by those up valley who wished to discourage prying eyes. Wadd or black lead (graphite to us) mined at Seathwaite had become a valuable commodity. Any tall story that ensured its isolation was to the benefit of the smugglers intent on purloining copious amounts to ship out on packhorses at dead of night. To maintain the sense of imminent danger, travellers were warned to keep silent whilst in the vicinity of the Jaws lest the echo from voices should bring a welter of rocks crashing down.

The Walk

Our walk begins from Grange-in-Borrowdale. Once an outlying farm, the settlement expanded in the 13th century as the administrative base for the monks who ran the Furness Abbey agricultural estate in the valley. Today it represents the epitome of Lakeland charm and is known more for the distinctive twin bridges that provide access to the single main street.

Take a stroll along the road for about 100 metres and turn left at the café, thus gaining the access road that serves Hallows Farm. After a quarter mile, branch left off this road along a rough track following the edge of woodland down to the river bank. At the big bend where Broadslack Gill merges with the Derwent, two footbridges allow easy progress along the river trail.

Beyond a fence stile, the path crosses an open glade before slanting left to accompany a wall up through Low Hows Wood. Watch for a gap in the wall and then continue along to the abandoned slate quarry below Castle Crag. Leave the main path to climb up to the system of caves that present the appearance of an apartment block.

Perhaps that is what attracted Millican Dalton to make the caves his summer residence during the inter-war years. The lower cave was forsaken due to its propensity for harbouring the wet stuff. In consequence, our intrepid hero chose the pair of caves at a higher level which he utilised as living quarters and bed chamber, the latter being referred to as the 'attic'.

On the November day I arrived, with rain falling heavier than inside a manic car wash, the inner sanctum was completely dry. Not a splash had penetrated, leaving the accommodation cosy and inviting. Or it would have been had not the previous occupants (Hallowe'en revellers judging by the

Millican Dalton's cave below Castle Crag

redundant pumpkins) left their rubbish cluttering an otherwise idyllic nook.

Although a devil-may-care luminary, Millican ensured that his time spent in Borrowdale was comfortable and snug. Cooking on a home-made fireplace, his meals were apparently of a high standard and he remained a vegetarian until his death in 1947. One could always ascertain when he was at home by the plume of smoke snaking up through the tree cover.

A frustrated member of the commuting herd, he threw off the tiresome yoke of convention to pursue a lifestyle that most people can only dream about. Much of his time was involved exploring and leading parties around the local fells. He eked out a frugal livelihood making tents and rucksacks, 'Professor of Adventure' being an apt designation he readily encouraged.

Punting on a Heath Robinson-type raft on Derwent Water continued to provide much pleasure for this eccentric Robinson Crusoe well into his 70s. Each summer he would return and once again take up residence under Castle Crag. Winters found him in the warmer south of England, where he finally passed away at the ripe age of 80 years, a man who had discovered how to live his own life freed from the shackles of society's expectations.

Above the entrance to the cave, a poignant philosophy is carved into the stone thus:

Don't!! Waste worrds, jump to conclusions.

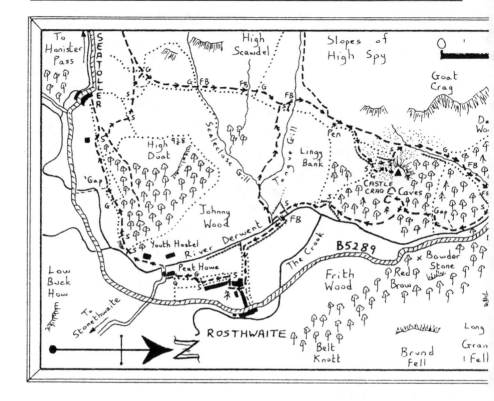

The double 'r' was intended as a private joke between the 'Professor' and his Scottish friend who did the work. Perhaps some knowledgeable reader could enlighten this ignorant soul as to its meaning.

Return to the main track, continuing south to the edge of the wood. Once over a stile the path circles left towards the river, which it then accompanies to a gate. Just beyond this lies New Bridge and a choice of routes.

Those suddenly recalling an urgent appointment with their tax inspector should take the winding path that loops up Lingy Bank alongside Tongue Gill to join the old road higher up, thence returning to Grange.

More stalwart Goliaths will cock a snook at such excuses, crossing the bridge and continuing along the far side of the Derwent until it slants left towards Rosthwaite. After passing the first farm at the edge of the village, turn right along a cul-de-sac until a line of new bungalows is reached. Bear right then left over a stile to follow the rear wall of these homes along to another stile at the end of the field. Mount the stile and lean half right towards a gate in the wall, after which a clear path leads round to Peat Howe. The right of

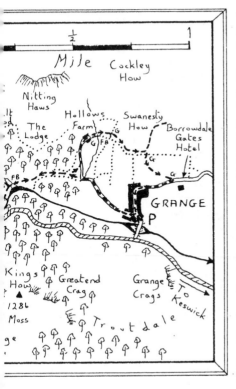

way cuts left of this building to reach an access lane leading to the youth hostel.

Our route passes left of this wooden building to cross a stile at the far side adjacent to the river. Take special care when negotiating the bare slabs of rock sliding down into the river over the next 100 metres. Another stile then brings us into a walled passage hemmed in by the lower edge of Johnny Wood. Go through a gate to cross open ground, with the wall still on your left. After a gap at the far end, stick with the wall – now on the right. Slipping through a pair of wide wall gaps and near to the large house of Glaramara, the path once again reverts to the opposite side of the wall via a stile.

Another 100 metres on the approach to Seatoller, cut back up to the right on a major track heading into Johnny Wood. When another track swerves sharp left, take it for no more than 50 metres, then slant up the steepening valley side along a clear, grass causeway through the bracken. An old road is soon joined rising from Seatoller. Take note of a wall stile ahead, then accompany the ancient highway uphill and through another stile.

The clear route now continues ahead on a westerly course bound for Honister Pass. At a signposted crossing of trails, our way lies up the grass bank ahead to a gate near the left wall corner. Having joined the old road from Grange, head north along this fine route as it contours the lower slopes of High Scawdel. The distinctive pyramid of Castle Crag provides a clear objective to aim for.

Just beyond a sheep pen, leave the main track if the ascent of Castle Crag is considered worthy of the extra effort at this latter stage of the walk. Those who regularly consume three shredded wheat will exhibit no hesitation. Climb a thin trail under the lower crags and over a broken wall to reach a fence. Follow this to its terminus, where a stile is crossed, followed immediately by another over a wall. The narrow trod snakes ahead, soon reaching the loose debris from past slate quarrying days. Care is needed on the steeply canting scree path.

Once the higher level is gained through a scattering of larches, it is easy to see how such a natural stronghold controlled access to Upper Borrowdale. No visible signs of the original earthworks remain, the summit having acquired the status of a war memorial. A fitting tribute to the men of Borrowdale who succumbed during the Great War, and also for those who went before in a more turbulent period of its history.

On the day your doughty guide battled his way to an heroic conquest of the Castle in the Sky, it was the natural enemies of wind and rain that attempted to thwart his ambition. Suffice it to say that a fearless disregard for personal comfort overrode all else in pursuit of the finest of walks to offer his readers.

After returning to the wall stile, bear right down a clear path to another crossing a fence, followed instantly by a rotting ladder. Descend rough slopes to a lower wall and then go through a gap to rejoin the main track. Hemmed in by soaring buttresses on either side, the rough trail soon drops to enter the confines of Dalt Wood by a gate. It then accompanies Broadslack Gill down to its merger with the Derwent.

Retrace your steps to the access road serving Hollows Farm and head left. Pass through the farmyard to emerge on a field track at the far side which soon crosses a small bridge. Stick with this clear path through a gate and then alongside a wall on the right. When the path bends left to round High Close Wood, go through a gate on the right and follow the thin trod down across the lower pastures to the Manesty road. You will emerge through a gate opposite the Borrowdale Gates Hotel. Swing right, back down the road for the return to Grange.

Walk 17

Kirkby Stephen: Snared by the Devil

Mystery:	Church on the Hill, GR 730097
Distance:	7½ miles
Total Height Climbed:	800 feet (244 metres)
Nearest Centre:	Crosby Garrett
Start and Finish:	There is plenty of suitable roadside parking in Crosby Garrett. I chose to park on the road adjacent to St Andrew's Church.
Map:	Ordnance Survey Pathfinder 607, Tebay and Kirkby Stephen.

Located in a sleepy hollow, Crosby Garrett occupies the site of an ancient lake produced from the glacial meltdown following the last Ice Age. Stone Age colonists recognised the fertile nature of the terrain hereabouts and have left visible evidence of their presence in the form of diverse settlement outlines.

The isolated nature of the village becomes readily apparent to those approaching from the south and west, direct access being forestalled by an extensive limestone plateau. Hampered by a narrow, waterlogged road which fords Scandel Beck, casual visitors are a distinct rarity. In consequence, you will be guaranteed a degree of solitude on this remote walk that few others are able to match.

A linear village ranged along either side of a narrow stream, the religious grounding of the community is clear from the provision of three churches in such a small community. Dominating the whole from a lofty vantage point atop Church Hill, St Andrew's is one of the oldest such establishments in Westmorland.

In those distant times when life was rather precarious, and arguments concerning land trespass were a tad more forceful, the hill acted as a lookout post to watch for approaching insurgents. Built with defence as well as spiritual aims in mind, the vulnerable sheltered here whilst their menfolk went to meet the challenge.

This sturdy house of God presents a simple yet dignified image, catering to the ecclesiastical needs of an enduring congregation. The red sandstone arch dissecting the interior testifies to its archaic pedigree. But it is the hagioscope that is the most intriguing element. A square opening cut through this inner wall at an angle, enables the entire congregation to follow the proceedings at the altar.

Legend suggests that in the murky depths of time, the first church was meant for erection at the bottom of the hill. All the materials were gathered ready to begin construction. But next morning, upon waking, it was discovered that all the stone and timber had been moved to the top. This was before Jeremy Beadle had appeared on the scene. So who was the rascally prankster?

None other than his satanic majesty. Old Nick himself had shifted the lot in his leather apron during the hours of darkness. His intention? By making the climb too difficult for the old and infirm, he hoped to weaken their resolve, thus enticing more recruits into the Devil's kitchen. On the day I passed this way, both old and young alike were struggling manfully up the steeply canting path inside the church yard. The horned demon had grossly underestimated the spirit inherent within the village, thus promulgating the triumph of light over darkness.

It has been mooted that this story symbolises the conflict betwixt long held pagan beliefs and the newly emergent Christian doctrines that marked the Dark Ages. Almost certainly, the manmade dais on which the church resides was the site of early heathen worship. Perhaps the simple village

Hagioscope in St Andrew's Church

folk considered it more expedient to appease both ideologies. And who are we to blame them?

The name Crosby Garrett, meaning 'crosses belonging to Gerard', certainly has religious overtones. Although the cleric in question must himself have been as reclusive as the village, no record of his presence having survived. And once the village has been vacated, think well on the fact that no other 'living' soul is likely to be encountered in the surrounding countryside.

The Walk

After walking up the village street towards the viaduct which carries the Settle-Carlisle railway, bear right at the telephone kiosk. Bend to the right again and watch for a stile on the left giving access to a footbridge crossing the railway. Continue ahead with a hedge on the right to the far end, where a gap takes you into the adjoining field, again on the right.

Spot a narrow stile offset to the right in the facing hedge, after which a short stroll will bring you to another giving entry to Ladle Lane. This rough-walled track provides farm access to the intake fields supporting sheep during the winter months.

Towards the end of the lane the left boundary is fenced, the track tapering appreciably and becoming stony underfoot. At the end, it takes a sharp left but a gate enables a westerly course to be maintained. Cresting the brow of the broad ridge between Crosby Garrett and Potts Valley, keep straight ahead to arrive at Newclose Lane.

A pair of gates on either side of this rough-walled track allow continued progress, following the wall on your left. Over a wall stile, the right of way makes a gradual descent to the field corner, where a further stile deposits you in the adjoining field on the left. Hereafter, the grass flanks steepen as you descend to the valley bottom and the abandoned farmstead of Potts.

Turn south, following this limestone gorge upstream. Another pair of stiles are soon left behind in this lonely, virtually unknown dale. Few other such examples remain in Cumbria. Only the bleating sheep and chattering beck disturb the stillness of the air. Tranquil and serene, words fail to capture this entrancing portrait of rustic harmony that remains inherently Westmorland.

What more could the solitary walker need? Especially when a watery autumn sun illuminates the dusky tints of fall, the walk towards the lone sheepfold must surely have contributed to what the Eden Valley is all about.

South of Hazzler Brow Scar, the valley opens out whilst making a wide sweep to the right. Where the path divides after crossing a level, grassy

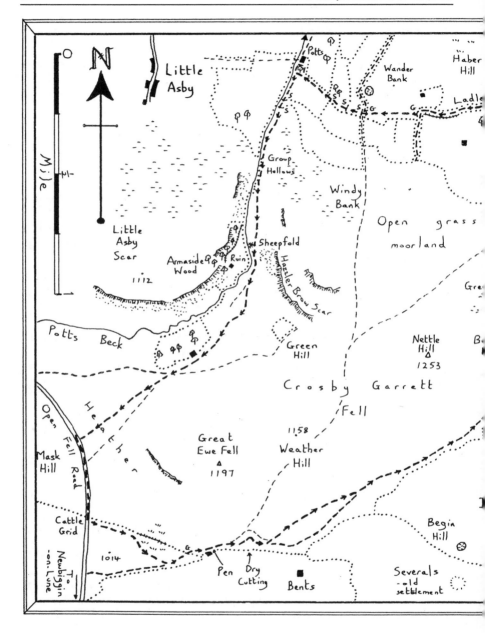

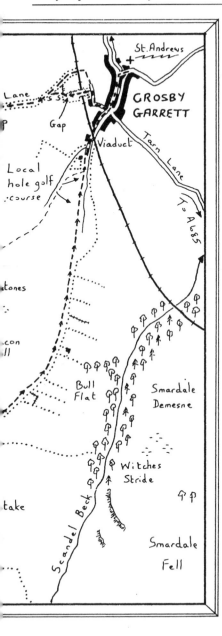

promenade, fork left up a gentle incline. As height is gained, it homes in to meet the upper edge of a walled enclosure dotted with clumps of trees.

At its far end, keep straight ahead along the most prominent track heading generally south-west. After a half mile, the open fell road traversing this bleak heather moor is joined. Slant left in the direction of Newbiggin-on-Lune for a quarter mile until a cattle grid is reached. Leave the road here, swinging left alongside a wall. The path detours around Ewefell Mire, returning to pass through a gate, beyond which is a barn and sheep pen. Circle round a dry depression characteristic of limestone terrain to fork left up a higher, level track, bearing away from the intake wall.

Once Bents Farm is passed below on the right, the path climbs gradually, veering in to accompany the wall once again. Stick with this obvious guide, on a strengthening track all the way back to Crosby Garrett. On the final approach to the village, take note of the ingenious use made of the rough fellside where a nine-hole golf course has been engineered. An inspired product of local initiative, it is clearly a well utilised amenity. One can only speculate as to where the 'aprés--golf' celebrations are held.

Continue down the hill and under the viaduct to gain the village street from the south. The devil was doubtless thwarted in his tenacious recruiting drive hereabouts because his inveterate foe had already laid claim to the area. Certainly this very special walk possesses all the ingredients that are more in keeping with heavenly guidance than with Old Nick's rapacious yardstick.

Walk 18

Glenridding: Beware O'Aira

Mystery:	The White Lady GR 400205
Distance:	5 miles
Total Height Climbed:	1150 feet (350 metres)
Nearest Centre:	Glenridding
Start and Finish:	Park in the lakeside pull-in off the A592, immediately opposite the fence stile marking the start of this walk.
Map:	Ordnance Survey English Lakes, 1:25 000, north-east area

Rising out of England's second largest lake, the sprawling upland moor of Gowbarrow Fell contrasts markedly with the sublime tranquillity of the wooded parkland skirting the lake shore. Although of an irregular configuration, this modest fell issues a salutary warning to the many tourists who mill about on the lower slopes in the vicinity of Aira Force. A scattering of low crags combine to ensure that Gowbarrow is no delicate hillock to be treated with impunity. And hidden amongst the trees cloaking the southern flank, the savage buttress of Yew Crag has long been the preserve of the climbing fraternity.

This rural idyll has oft stimulated debate from Wordsworth aficionados as to whether this was indeed the locale for his most celebrated ode. Daffodils certainly line the placid shores of the lake in springtime. They so impressed the poet's sister Dorothy that she penned a graphic description in her journal. It was to be a further two years before William recalled how he 'wandered lonely as a cloud'. At the time, he appeared to be more impressed by the inverted reflection of Lyluph's Tower observed in the balmy reach of Ullswater. A false impression, certainly if one obtains a rear view of the structure. Built in 1780 as a hunting lodge by the Duke of Norfolk, the crenellated façade is then revealed for the shallow folly that it is.

The Walk

Cross the road from the gravel pull-in and take the path slanting left up into the confines of the lower woods. The route acts as a dividing line separating the natural, open woodland from the gloomy uniformity of conifers. Closing with a fence on the left, we emerge from the tree cover as the path slices through thick bracken.

A stone memorial seat should be admired, but not tested until our return at a later stage in the walk. Occupying centre stage in the open field on the left, the true nature of Lyulph's Tower can be seen close at hand. Soon after, the path merges with the main route skirting Gowbarrow and continues ahead towards Aira Beck.

It is here that the primary objective of our expedition can first be heard:

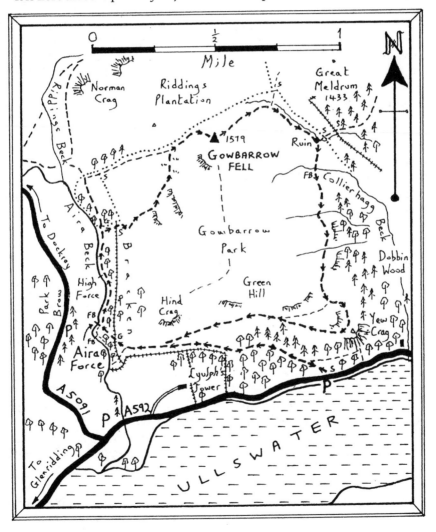

> *'List, ye who pass by Lyulph's Tower*
> *At eve, how softly then,*
> *Doth Aira Force, that torrent hoarse,*
> *Speak from the woody glen.'*

Beyond a gate, drop down to the footbridge spanning the cataclysmic ravine. Mere words cannot do justice to the powerful sight that assails the senses as the foaming deluge thunders over the rock bar. Better to descend the railed flight of stone steps to the lower bridge where the true majesty of this awesome cataract is displayed in all its pristine glory.

Ensconced within the sylvan grotto, one can but stand and marvel in open-mouthed wonder at the 25-metre waterfall plunging deep into the rocky chasm. Visited by generations of sightseers, even the provision of a purpose-built stairway has failed to tarnish the mystical allure emanating from this startling fissure.

For here it was that a story of tragic consequences was played out to the end in true romantic fashion. Casting back to medieval times, a certain Lady Emma resided in a castle just above the present Lyulph's Tower and fell hopelessly in love with a gallant knight errant. But as with many such adventurers, he spent much of his time in pursuit of honour and glory on the battlefields of the Middle East.

Restless for his return, Lady Emma began sleepwalking and often found herself in the vicinity of Aira Force, where the couple had spent many happy hours. On his next visit, Sir Eglamore was nearing the falls when he espied a wraithlike apparition in the wooded enclave. Not knowing if this was indeed his loved one, the knight made a stealthy approach lest he frighten the girl.

Wordsworth was so entranced by the story that he immortalised it in *The Somnambulist*. And as the bold chevalier laid his hand upon the lady's arm whilst she stood poised upon the brink,

> *'The soft touch snapped the thread*
> *Of slumber – shrieking back she fell,*
> *And the stream whirled her down the dell*
> *Along its foaming bed'*

A more recent report comes from De Quincey. He spoke of an intrepid woman of independent mind who would often venture into wild places on her own. One day she determined to explore the fearsome confines of Aira Beck by climbing up the perilous gorge. Finding herself in difficulties with no apparent means of escape from the aerial dungeon, the poor woman naturally became concerned for her well-being.

Suddenly, up ahead, she perceived a veiled figure in white muslin beckoning her onward. Discovering a route that had previously eluded her,

Miss Smith came up to the stranger who proved to be her own sister. The sinuous presence pointed the way to safety and then immediately vanished. When the perplexed woman arrived home and related the events, the astonished sister was at pains to deny that that she had ever left the house at all that day.

After duly concluding that Miss Smith's daring exploit was a rather ambitious feat best left to expert climbers, make your way back up to the top bridge. From here, head upstream in the direction of High Force. Climb above an enclosed dell located a little higher upstream. Although not in the same league as the main fall, it is nonetheless an impressive water-cut fissure in the bedrock.

Still further up Aira Beck is located the more accessible cascade of High Force, one of numerous along the intriguing length of this action-packed watercourse. Soon after, the path reaches a gate in the wall enclosing a small wood. We leave Aira Beck at this point and strike uphill alongside the wall until a fence is reached.

Cross a stile and make your way up an intermittent yet easy to follow path that climbs above this bracken-clad western flank of Gowbarrow Fell. If you are following the correct route, it should slant left to merge with another accompanying the cross-fell wall up from Aira Beck at a marshy depression. Stick with the wall until the summit is neared. Then lean right, away from the wall to reach the stone trig column atop the fell.

Few of those encountered in the valley below make it this far, so your only companions are likely to be of the woolly variety. A languid air of remoteness pervades the heathery swell and offers a pleasing dais from which to scan the valley of King Ulf.

After this relaxing sojourn, head east, parallel to the wall until it swings south-east. The path does likewise eventually, arriving at the ruins of an old shooting lodge. Here we join the main right of way linking the parks of Swinburn and Gowbarrow. Heading south, our course crosses a deep gully via a newish footbridge and thence meanders across the acclivitous eastern flank of the fell.

This path makes for an exhilarating and airy walk above the forested lower slopes enclosing Collierhagg Beck. A sharp left wheel is soon followed by an abrupt swing to the right as the cairned eminence above Yew Crag is approached. Cross the fence stile to ogle the precipitous drop into the woods below the crag, which remains hidden from view up here. An official path that once afforded a rapid if tenuous descent to valley level has been placed out-of-bounds to walkers by the National Trust due to a dangerous rock fall. Take heed of this warning and continue along the main route back in the direction of Aira Beck.

Gently graded and direct, it converges with the lower path opposite

Lyulph's Tower. Make a sharp left here, returning to the main road along our outward path. A walk of stark contrasts, the vibrant display of claustrophobic intensity around the fall surrenders to open moorland, and a more relaxed, yet still exhilarating atmosphere.

Aira Force plunges down a constricted ravine

Walk 19

Keswick: Lonely is the Hermit

Mysteries:	St Herbert's Island, GR 259213, the Floating Island, GR 2619
Distance:	5 miles
Total Height Climbed:	1300 feet (396 metres)
Nearest Centre:	Portinscale
Start and Finish:	Numerous roadside pull-ins are available around the hairpin bend at the northern extremity of the Cat Bells ridge.
Map:	Ordnance Survey English Lakes, 1:25 000, north-west area

Broadest of the lakes, Derwent Water is renowned for its tranquillity. Eminently charming, it is regarded as The Queen of Lakes and remains a regal aristocrat in all seasons. An irregular shoreline assists in creating a heavenly environment that has lost none of its allure due to the ravages of commercial exploitation.

Discrete and shaded beneath the overhang of an indigenous woodland fringe, numerous shingle bays can be explored at one's leisure. Way back in 1769, Dr John Brown paid an artistic tribute to the lake by describing it as the epitome of 'beauty, horror and immensity' – referring to the circlet of naked cliffs that rose up on either bank. The view most assuredly transfixed early tourists, who were in awe of the majestic scene.

Contemporary prints of the day always tended towards exaggeration when attempting to depict the surging plane of saw-toothed peaks under a lowering sky. Yet even today, when a grey shroud blankets the surrounding fells, Derwent Water and her attendant entourage hold no fears for the walker who revels in his own company.

Dotted with islands that each have a story to unfold, the secluded inlets are readily accessible by a regular ferry service plying across the placid reach and calling at tiny landing stages en route. Largest and most central is St Herbert's Island, best observed from the ridge of Skelgill Bank whilst descending from Catbells. Being the focus of this mysterious walk, the ascent of Catbells is recommended in order to more fully appreciate the configuration of the lake and its island retinue. Walla Crag, controlling the eastern prospect on the far shore, is itself draped in a mystical fascination that is the subject of Walk 21.

Known to have led a solitary life in the 7th century on the island that bears his name, St Herbert existed by catching fish and growing his own vegetables. A devout monk, his life was dedicated to prayer and meditation. He would have attracted little attention had he not struck up a remarkable friendship with St Cuthbert who was the Bishop of Lindisfarne. Cuthbert visited him on the island once each year to share in his devotions. The two companions made a pact to leave this mortal life at one and the same time. And so it came to pass that on April 13th 687, Herbert died on his island whilst Cuthbert expired on Farne Island off the coast of Northumberland.

Renowned as a major ecclesiastical figure in the Dark Ages, the latter's remains are interred within Durham Cathedral. Nobody is quite sure as to where Herbert is buried. Due in no small measure to his stoic resolve, he did, however, assume a degree of prominence within religious circles.

The ruins of a chapel constructed in the 14th century can still be seen on a clear day. The Bishop of Crosthwaite initiated an annual pilgrimage to the chapel to celebrate the anniversary of St Herbert's death. Adjacent to the chapel is a tiny, stone grotto erected by Sir Wilfrid Lawson a century ago, his own personal tribute to this singular priest.

No doubt one of the fish caught by Herbert was the vendace, today one of the rarest fish in the country and only found in Bassenthwaite and Derwent Water. Under threat from other more common species such as roach and ruffe, every effort is being made to prevent its extinction. Scientists from the Institute of Freshwater Ecology are at present studying ways of realigning the natural balance of aquatic life within the two lakes, so far without much success.

On the day I arrived to view Herbert's domain, the brilliant tones beloved of picture postcard photographers had faded to an indigenous slate grey. Billowing cumulus hovered ominously above the rampant peaks, casting a pall over the halcyon calm of the lake. Doubtless our holy recluse would have welcomed the frequency of such climatic vagaries to prevent any distraction from his godly commitment. Such was the strength and influence of his dedication that sainthood was conferred and the annual commemorative mass inaugurated. Even Wordsworth was impressed by St Herbert, expressing his regard poetically:

> '.........a self-secluded man,
> After long exercise in social cares,
> And offices humane, intent to adore
> The Deity with undistracted mind,
> And meditate on everlasting things
> In utter solitude.'

The Walk

From the pull-ins abutting the Skelgill hairpin, take a stroll along the wall that heads north-east down through the woods to meet the access road serving Hause End. Turn right along the metalled highway for 100 metres before slanting left along a rough track. Pass behind the outdoor pursuits centre, with a strip steel fence on the left, until a stile is reached.

Fork left here off the main track, which continues ahead into the wooded enclave of Brandelhow Park. Our path closes with the tree-fringed edge of the lake, crossing a fence stile near to Otterbield Bay. The path angles left into a short, fenced corridor with a stile at its end. Continue ahead to the shoreline and a landing stage where another stile is crossed.

Maintain this southward course along the edge of the lake, glimpsing the noble upthrust of Walla Crag on the opposite shore. Can there be any lakeside walk that upstages this for its serenity and assurance that all is well with the world?

Beyond the next landing stage, the Brandelhow track forks in from the right. The main route leans away from the water's edge to circle behind an old mine and then crosses a fence stile into Brandelhow Bay. Pass in front of the boathouses, aiming for a gate at the far end of the beach.

Stroll south down a fenced lane. Where the main track continues ahead into Manesty Park, take a left alongside a fence, returning to the lakeside adjacent to Otter Island. Meandering through the open woodland, head south-east towards the end of the lake. Log footbridges provide a dry walkway through the marshy tracts. These are followed by extended plank duckboards which bring us into the grassy pastures at the lake's end.

Mystery and romance surround this part of Derwent Water. One might well be lucky enough to espy a will-o'-the-wisp known as The Floating Island emerging from the reedy tract. It appears about once every three years, but only when there has been a prolonged spell of hot weather.

Rotting vegetation that has settled on the lake bed, at this point about one metre deep, rises to the surface. Made buoyant through the release of marsh gas, the phenomenon only occurs after the underlying ground has been allowed to heat up. Once thought to have been a section of solid earth that had broken away, this theory was scuppered when bubbles caused by the gaseous emissions were observed. In the early years following its discovery, people were known to have picnicked on the uneven surface. Unfortunately, on the day I passed this way, no strange addition to the lake furniture could be seen, nor is it recorded on the Ordnance Survey map. If anybody has chanced to experience this elusive phenomenon, I would welcome their observations.

Fork right, away from the lake, along a grass causeway aiming towards the walled stand of conifers that mark the southern limits of Manesty Park.

Cross a stile to follow the edge of the tree cover and soon thereafter, another. Close with a fence homing in from the left which chaperones the track to its convergence with the Grange road. Head right, up the lane to Manesty. Immediately beyond the farm, fork left up a clear track which soon swings sharply left to mount the steep flank of Manesty Brow.

Beyond a fence stile, continue uphill, but avoid the obvious detour branching right towards the woods. Maintain a steady upward trek marking the higher level route that contours across this eastern slope of Cat Bells. Should the increasingly steep pull be proving too much for jaded muscles, escape is at hand along this old mine road. Certainly an excellent return to Hause End for those awaiting their telegram from the Palace.

Those seeking a closer acquaintance with their maker should keep on up the path towards a distinct rock step. As height is gained, severe boot erosion and unnecessary short cutting from the track below has led to the erection of fencing to channel the pathway. The upper section pursues a zigzag course prior to its arrival at Hause Gate. Something of a contradiction in view of the double epithet, both words referring to a pass in the hills.

Head north up the gently shelving ridge, on to the distinctive pyramid of Cat Bells. The name is thought to have originated from the western crags known as Mart Bield where the area was populated by an abundance of martens. Wild cats had disappeared in the early 1800s whereas the less aggressive marten survived for another century. Tourists knew

Catbells viewed from across Derwentwater

nothing of these elusive creatures, but were well acquainted with cats. And so, due to the influence from outsiders, Mart Bield became Cat Bield, and finally the universally recognised Cat Bells.

Crowned with a circlet of grey crags, the domed summit offers a magnificent prospect north across the Vale of Keswick to Skiddaw. Yet how can

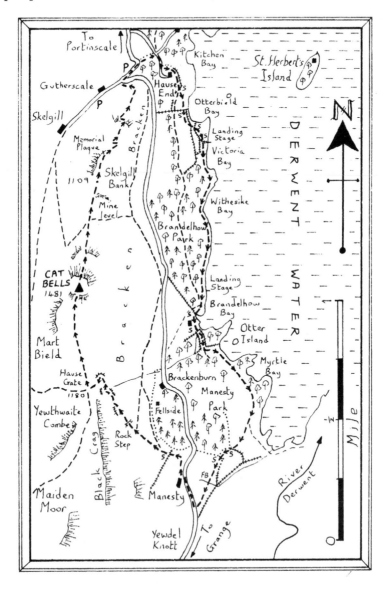

any view be chosen as superior, surrounded as it is by such breathtaking scenery? No other fell in Lakeland attracts such a broad spectrum of visitors. Everybody who aspires to mountain conquest makes this highly-charged ascent once in their lives. In consequence, it is better to make your own pilgrimage out of season, when all is quiet and Cat Bells can be yours alone.

The steep descent of the rocky north face adds a certain piquancy to this unique challenge. But care is needed on the exposed turrets for those unused to the rigours associated with rough terrain. At the base of the main tower, a contrasting amble follows along the grassy, level ridge of Skelgill Bank. This is when the profile of St Herbert's Island can be observed properly and at one's ease.

After crossing a brief depression at the upper level of the old Brandley Mine, the final descent of the ridge begins. Passing an isolated outcrop, take note of the tablet anchored securely in memory of a certain Thomas Arthur Leonard. Below, a series of zigzags with fence accompaniment quickly returns us to the road hairpin above Hause End.

No other lake displays such bewitching allure and calm detachment to seduce both mind and body. Savour to the full this charisma whilst imbibing the mythical lore which is never far away.

Walk 20

Shap: East of Haweswater

Mysteries:	The Vanishing Corpse GR 485119, Hugh Laithes Pike GR 503152 and Wallow Crag GR 495151.
Distance:	8 miles
Total Height Climbed:	900 feet (274 metres)
Nearest Centre:	Bampton Grange
Start and Finish:	One mile before the end of the valley road at Mardale Head, and immediately north of where the old corpse road begins, there is ample roadside parking space available.
Map:	Ordnance Survey English Lakes, 1:25 000, north-east area

'What the human persona avoids, nebulous shadows embrace with relish.'
GKD 1997

Unlike the rampaging fell country that clusters around Mardale Head, the undulating moorland to the east of Haweswater is devoid of human activity. Paths are limited and still in their original condition. Much of the terrain is rough grazing, the sole preserve of wandering woollies, or itinerant walkers in search of quirky phenomena. So as you pass through the gate at the start of the old corpse road, think well on the purpose of this ancient route. Until 1729, when the church at Mardale Green was erected, deceased villagers were conveyed over Mardale Common and down into Swindale. From there, it was an easier continuation to their final resting place in consecrated ground at Shap.

One story involves a murderer whose heinous crime went undetected during his lifetime. The felon clearly went to his maker with a guilty conscience, the heavens erupting in tempestuous fury whilst his body was in transit along the corpse road. Beset with terror, the panicky horse stampeded with the laden coffin strapped to its back. When it finally reappeared three months later, the coffin was still firmly in place. By this time the blackguard's skulduggery had come to light, and some say this was a belated punishment enacted by the victim's spirit.

The Walk

Mount the trail that zigzags up the initially steep cant alongside the tumbling spume of Rowantreethwaite Beck. Could this be the longest appellation of any stream in Lakeland? When the gradient eases to circumvent the marshy source of this meandering rill, a series of marker posts line the route. Intended as guides during the blanched depths of winter, accompany them to the highest point of the track before it descends into Swindale.

Leaving the solid presence of the corpse road, head due north across pathless and rather obscure terrain to reach Woof Crag a half mile distant. As the north face of this craggy outcrop involves a sheer cliff, bird-like impressions are not to be recommended if onward progress is to be maintained. A further half mile to the north-east will bring you to the substantial cairn atop Hare Shaw.

Although little above the surrounding reach of knolls, it does attain the distinction of being the highest point between Swindale and Mardale. There is nothing sufficiently engrossing to keep us here, so head north down the grass-clad sweep to reach the boundary wall surrounding Naddle Forest. Secluded and remote from casual acquaintance, few if any who motor down to Mardale Head will be aware that this tranquil valley even exists.

It is unfortunate that access is prohibited by North West Water, who have enclosed much of the valley as a wildlife preserve. Take note of the prominent addition to the far ridge for this is the nearest you can approach to Hugh Laithes Pike. The summit cairn marks the spot where the remains of a renowned local huntsman from yesteryear are supposed to be buried.

Jimmy Lowther was also known for his excessive drinking, which eventually killed him. While out riding in Mardale, he was thrown from his horse and died instantly from a broken neck without making his peace with God. Unable to settle, Jimmy's ghost haunted the neighbourhood, causing all manner of distress amongst the populace. In consequence, they eventually plucked up the courage to remove the bones and inter them on the remote hilltop of the pike. Secreted beneath a large stone, it was hoped that the spectral visitations would cease. And so it proved, although sitings of a freakish nature have been observed on occasion lurking about the fell top at dusk.

Follow the wall heading north-east past a lone chimney. The path improves below the craggy outcrop of Powley's Hill and passes through a gate close to a fenced sheep pen. A gradual ascent over Harper Hills will bring you to a small, enclosed reservoir. This is the only visible evidence that water from Swindale Beck is diverted into Haweswater.

Continue alongside the wall down to a walkers' crossroads. Bear left

*Solitary chimney above the Naddle Valley,
looking to Hugh Laithes Pike*

through a gate and follow the right of way down into the woodland that cloaks this side of the Naddle. Beyond the next gate, the path descends to the valley floor and over a fence stile to ford the beck close to an old dam.

Mount the facing bank through another gate to join the valley track. Head right through a gate to cross the yard of Naddle Farm. Take the gate on the left, passing a dog pound through the next gate to follow a wall around to the right. The overgrown path circles round the eastern shoulder of Hugh Laithes Pike, where much new fencing has been erected.

Pass through another gate prior to dropping down through natural woodland to gain the reservoir road. Take a left here for a half mile, keeping an eye open for the signposted path to Mardale Head. Initially slanting down alongside a fence to the old Boat House, the path accompanies the lake side for most of the way.

After the first half mile, the looming presence of Wallow Crag hovers in menacing fashion overhead. Marked by a chaotic splay of moss-shrouded boulders torn from the cliff face, here was enacted an occurrence of tragic consequence.

It concerns a Kentmere poet of some repute named Charles Williams. Not a normal, impish child, it was said 'a strange and wayward wight was he'. At the very moment of his birth, a massive rock tore free from the heights of Wallow Crag and ploughed into the valley below. According to his mother, this was an omen that her son was 'born to be drooned'. When still a thoughtful young man, he fell in love with Maria, whose gaiety and spirit enchanted the wistful poet, stimulating much of his writing. It was little wonder that he spent most of his treasured hours in the company of the lovely maiden.

But this courtship was brought to a mournful conclusion when Maria died from an unknown disease. Plunged into a wretched bout of despair, the distraught fellow became inconsolable. He took to wandering aimlessly for hours across the moors above Haweswater. He failed to return from one such trek and was found next morning close to the boulder that had tumbled from Wallow Crag.

Charles Williams drowned as his mother had predicted. Such an act of desperation to terminate his grief must have been planned if this final ode to his parting is to be believed:

> *And what is death, that I should dread*
> *To mingle with the silent dead?*
> *Tis but a pang – and pangs are o'er;*
> *A throb – and throbbing is no more;*
> *One struggle – and that one my last:*
> *A gasp – a groan – and all is past!*

Mere coincidence perhaps? Or was the fate of this sensitive bard preordained?

Continue along the narrow trail that slips neatly between road and reservoir. At this stage its course lies mainly through light tree cover. After a mile, the tall chimneys of Haweswater Hotel indicate that the halfway point down the lake has been reached. Two footbridges are crossed in fairly rapid succession thereafter.

As the reservoir tower is neared, cross straight over the access track and climb the banking up to the road wall ahead. The path then crosses a flight of stone steps leading down to the pier before entering a small wood of dense conifers. Passing between the wall and a fence, emerge at the far side after 100 metres to descend a sketchy trail through the bracken.

Soon improving, we then climb above a prominent crag overlooking the lake, but well below road level. A quarter mile further and the glowering upthrust of Whiteacre Crag is passed. On reaching the major lake feeder of Rowantreethwaite Beck, our route leaves the lakeside path to swing sharply left up the valley side to the road above.

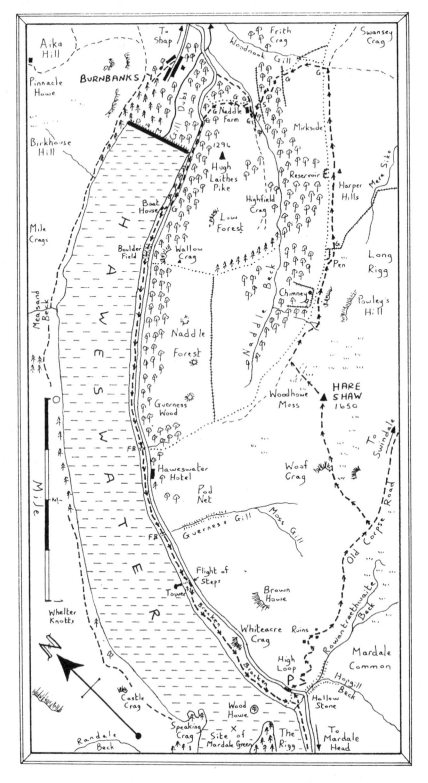

This must be the original start of the old corpse road from Mardale Green. Tucked between the surging prow of The Rigg and White Howe (now an island), the old village finally ended its association with the valley in 1936. Only in times of severe drought can the resurrected bones be investigated, as the plan of this drowned settlement becomes apparent.

Hidden secrets there are in abundance in this corner of Lakeland. Seek them out whilst enjoying a walk of unsurpassed charm and intrigue.

Walk 21

Keswick: Flight from Lord's Island

Mysteries:	The Ladies of Derwent Water GR 265219
Distance:	6 miles
Total Height Climbed:	1200 feet (366 metres)
Nearest Centre:	Keswick
Start and Finish:	The most obvious start would appear to be from the National Trust car park in Great Wood below Walla Crag. If you do not mind the most arduous climb being towards the end of this walk, then opt for my choice of route which starts from the pull-in just north of Castle Lane on the A591. This makes for an unusual walk and is much to be preferred.
Map:	Ordnance Survey English Lakes, 1:25 000, north-west area

In similar fashion to walk number 19, this outing also involves the past residents from one of Derwent Water's majestic islands. Certainly the stroll along the eastern shoreline can be adjudged of equal merit, the path encompassing a tortuous course around shingle-fringed bays. Even a busy weekend at the height of the season failed to curb my enthusiasm for this most delectable corner of Lakeland.

Popular without doubt, Derwent Water's regal demeanour has rightly earned the accolade of being dubbed 'Queen of the English Lakes'. Such recommendation could only have been reached with the climatic conditions in harmonious rapport. Unlike my previous visit, when Cat Bells and the surrounding fells lay smothered beneath a soused duvet, here was nature on her best behaviour, displaying her wares to perfection. In such surroundings, legends merely become light-hearted asides to mull over whilst casually reclining beneath some leafy bower, warmed by a late afternoon sun.

The Walk

Should you elect to begin this scintillating sojourn from the A591 (thoroughly recommended to avoid traffic problems), cross the road and take the signposted path heading south-west alongside a fence. Ahead, the easy, rolling fells rise gradually, culminating in the abrupt descent below Walla Crag, our ultimate destination. From here just a blip on the horizon, its true colours are only revealed from Derwent Water's verdant shores.

The immediate foreground is dominated by the boldly thrusting elbow of Pike, a knobbly outlier from the sprawling massif of Castlerigg Fell. After negotiating a stile, the grooved path slants left with another stile at the field end. A short, fenced corridor brings us to the next stile.

Beyond this and 100 metres ahead, mount a ladder stile to head due west alongside a wall to the next stile. Thereafter, the stony pathway funnels between a fence and wall down to the access lane serving Rakefoot. Take a left and then go immediately right over a stile hidden behind a hedge. Cross the next field and Brockle Beck by a narrow footbridge.

Bear right, following the chattering stream on a clear path as it filters down through the leafy glade towards Keswick. Beyond the radio mast and adjacent building 200 metres distant, lean sharp right into Springs Wood, but do not cross the bridge which will return you to Castlerigg Farm. Bear left alongside the beck, emerging on a road at Springs Farm.

Pass through a duo of gates and over Brockle Beck, which here swings west to feed into Derwent Water. Follow the road down an easy gradient, past a fringe estate of suburban dwellings. On the left of the lower section of the road after the dog-leg, watch for the fence/hedged footpath serving Castle Head.

Cross a stile and enter the lower confines of the wood. Initially left, our route then swings sharply right. Look out for the left turn which will bring you up to the fenced western edge of the wood. Keep ahead up a steepening incline, soon breaking from the tree cover into daylight on the rocky knoll of Castle Head. Laid out in front like a summer picnic table is the vista that has captivated visitors since the first tourists discovered the vale back in the 18th century. Truly an eye-caching experience – savour it to the full as countless generations have done before you.

Favoured by oarsmen and sailors alike, regular ferries ply the tranquil reach of Derwent Water and provide a useful means of return transit for tired walkers. But nothing which meanders between the verdant array of islands can quite match the simulated sea battles of Georgian Lakeland at the time of the naval wars with France.

Flotillas of gaily-bedecked boats scurried about amid 'terrible cannonades and dreadful discharges of musketry.' Followed by dancing and merrymaking 'til dawn, feverish enjoyment was had by all. A local scribe reported that the clamorous revelry could be heard in far-off Appleby!

Return to the fenced corner of Castle Head Wood, cutting down to the left in order to reach the Borrowdale Road. Cross to the far side and head left on the roadside path for 100 metres. Take a right turn into a link pathway serving Cockshot Wood. Faced with three equally clear trails, take the middle option across the thatched mound and thence along a fenced passage to gain the ferry landing stages.

Friars Crag, Derwent Water

Go left along the road, maintaining a southerly gait when it continues onward as a path to Friar's Crag. This scalloped promontory, capped by a shady arbour, provides a welcome seat from which to scan the southward prospect. Descending to the shingle beach, cross a fence stile. Lord's Island, completely swathed in a green mantle, holds the attention, being only 50 metres from the shore.

Concealed on the island lie the remains of an old manor house where the Lords of Derwent Water once held sway. And here occurred a pair of engaging mysteries to consider whilst circling around Strandshag Bay.

Last in a noble line of Derwent Water's aristocratic dignitaries, James was imprisoned in the Tower of London for supporting the Stuart dynasty in the early years of the 18th century. Confined on the island, his faithful wife did, however, succeed in escaping with her most treasured possessions. It was her intention to buy her husband's freedom, desperation forcing her to climb the precipitous west face of Walla Crag. Thereafter, the gully became known as Lady's Rake.

Unfortunately, the plan was doomed to failure and the good lord was executed in February of 1716. Coincidence or otherwise, a magnificent display of the aurora borealis that very night was afterwards referred to as Lord Derwent Water's Lights.

Enter the wooded enclave of The Ings through a gate and follow a clear path to its eastern extremity. Passing over a footbridge, slant right along the walled enclosure to leave by a gate at the far end. Here, join a gravel access track serving Stable Hills, located on the lake shore just beyond a gate and cattle grid.

As you stroll south, cast a nonchalant eye back to Lord's Isle in recollection of an earlier occurrence involving a less than charitable Lord of the Lake. This particular fiend was hated and feared by all who came across him, the blackguard even resorted to robbing his own friends. It was said that the proceeds of his iniquitous skulduggery were secured within a stronghold erected on Lord's Island.

For some unfathomable reason, his loving wife remained faithful to the rascally jackanapes, striving unsuccessfully to cure his evil practices. But this appears only to have spurred him to even greater excesses, until finally she could take no more. Whilst engaged on yet another of his plundering forays, she set fire to the cache of loot.

The fire spread rapidly and was soon beyond control. Fearing her husband's wrath, she fled by an unknown route up Walla Crag to stymie his pursuit. As before, it was the steep gully of Lady's Rake that procured an opportune flight. Cast an eye to the eastern profile of Walla Crag and the outline of the Rake can just be picked out among the new swathe of conifers. Definitely not a recommended route to follow.

South of Stable Hills, pass through a gate and bear left around another wooded eminence into Calfclose Bay. Beyond a footbridge, the path accompanies the pebbly shoreline. Look for a split boulder near the water's edge which has been sculpted with a mosaic on either face. Unusual to be sure, but I am reliably informed that other similar carvings are dotted around the lake.

Initially the path follows a fence, prior to angling right into the lower spread of Great Wood after crossing another small footbridge. Keeping parallel with the Borrowdale road for a quarter mile, almost to the edge of the wood, join the road where Cat Gill plunges down from the heights above to feed into Derwent Water.

Cross the road and go over a stile on the left side of the gill to begin the climbing phase of the walk. Keep close to the hissing torrent on a thin trail that winds ever upward through the dense undergrowth.

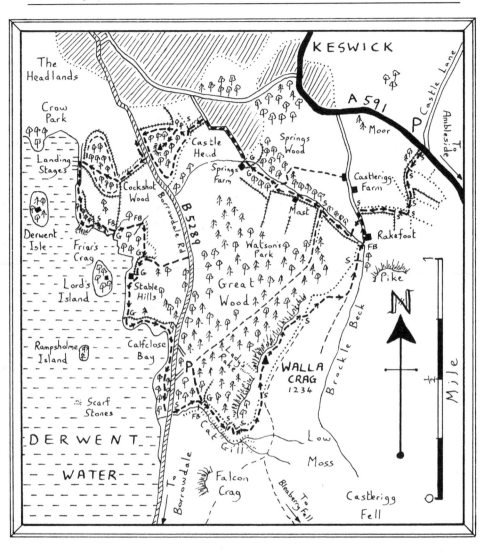

Soon, the upcoming track from the National Trust car park is joined. If this is your elected start, then begin reading from this point, the advantage being that the hard bit is over first.

Pass through a gate to use the reconstructed footpath that zigzags up the acclivitous flank, hemmed in by thick tree cover. Take note that the increasing depth of the ravine carved out by Cat Gill swings abruptly to the north-east. After the next stile, the sylvan canopy begins to thin out. Some years ago, I descended this track when it had degenerated into a severely eroded river of loose scree. The current, well-engineered replacement makes for a substantial improvement.

Follow the wall around to the left as it heads for the apex of Walla Crag. Stretching away to the east, the plateau of rough grassland culminates in the doughty prominence of Bleaberry Fell. Cross to the far side of the wall by a stile and make your way up to the highest point, perched on a dais overlooking Derwent Water's broad expanse.

Make time to sit awhile and ponder upon your ascent and that of the ladies of the Isle. And then, with feet firmly lodged in the 20th century, continue north from the summit along an exhilarating path that skirts the upper rim of the crags that give the fell its name. Cross back to the far side of the summit cross-wall through a stile and follow it downhill.

A detour forking right away from the wall is indicated by a row of posts. Aimed at allowing regeneration of a badly eroded section, the new, equally worn diversion merges with an old, grooved fell track. Continue down this to rejoin the wall in the emergent cutting occupied by Brockle Beck.

Beyond the next stile, cross to the far side of the beck by a footbridge adjacent to Rakefoot. Head down the road, keeping an eye open for the signposted route to Castlerigg Stone Circle. Thereafter, the outward half mile across the fields is retraced back to the A591.

Walk 22

Keswick: Thirsty Thirlmere's Hidden Haunts

Mysteries:	Armboth House GR 181172, Clark's Leap GR 320154
Distance:	7 miles
Total Height Climbed:	1200 feet (366 metres)
Nearest Centre:	Keswick
Start and Finish:	An official car park on the shores of Thirlmere at Armboth.
Map:	Ordnance Survey English Lakes, 1:25 000, north-west area

From the journals of early travellers penned more than a century ago, it would appear that Thirlmere has altered in character more than any other lake. Haweswater certainly has changed for ever, but at least its slopes were left in a natural state. Not so Thirlmere, which was the first valley to assuage the thirst of Manchester's burgeoning populace.

In addition to the devouring of its twin lakes, massed ranks of conifers were planted. Marching in file up the steep fellsides, they now possess all the uniformity of a Roman legion with none of the charisma. Certainly Wordsworth and his contemporaries would have been horrified at the changes wrought here in the name of progress.

Today the valley lies silent, cocooned in its own green chrysalis. Most people hurry by along the main artery bound for Keswick, offering barely a glance towards the turgid waters. And this is where Thirlmere scores heavily.

Largely abandoned by the majority of visitors, it provides a secluded environment remote from interruption with a lakeside walk of the highest quality. Above the forest boundary on the western flank, the bleak moorland wilderness affords the solitary walker the opportunity to commune with nature in the raw. But be warned that the saturated plateau will test the proofing qualities of the most impervious boots. A winter visit when the ground has frozen harder than a stale rock bun must, therefore, be recommended.

Access to the fells above is strictly limited to a few gaps in the forest curtain. Armboth is the best choice in view of a clear right of way passing over the summit of High Tove down to the hamlet of Watendlath. Not to mention a macabre history that will set teeth a-chattering and bones a-trembling.

On the shoreline close to the car park can be found the footings of the old boathouse that belonged to Armboth Farm. Demolished in 1894 when the valley was flooded, Armboth was once a thriving community. All that remains is the enigmatic Monkey Puzzle Tree, a Chilean Pine imported by a past landowner. Aloof in its own personal glade, this uniquely shaped conifer stands in haughty disdain of the lesser plantains introduced by the water board. Easily missed by the casual observer, it can be found 50 metres south of the car park along the shore path.

Armboth was reputed to be the most haunted house in Lakeland following the untimely demise of the farmer's daughter at Hallowe'en. Thrust into the grasping clutches of the dark waters, some say by her betrothed, she drowned on the night before her wedding. Nobody ever discovered the real perpetrator of the foul deed, but thereafter, on every Hallowe'en, a poltergeist caused all manner of unearthly shenanigans. Bells would ring, lights flashed and furniture rocked. Even the wedding table was laid to await the resurrection of the bride from her watery grave.

Thirlmere: foundations of Armboth House revealed during a recent drought

Such ghostly happenings engendered a host of fearful superstitions throughout the district and beyond. It was thought 'that on a certain night all the fugitive spirits whose bodies were destroyed in unavenged crime assembled at Armboth House'. Whatever the truth, here is one cautious soul who has no plans to be abroad in the vicinity at Hallowe'en.

The Walk

Following a cursory investigation of the Armboth environs, take the path signposted to Watendlath. Pass through a stile and aim for the obvious wall gap after crossing the stone footbridge over Middlesteads Gill close by a sheep pen. The path then climbs steadily with a wall on your left which soon gives way to a substantial fence.

Erected for the purpose of keeping the deer inside a manageable tract, you will be lucky indeed to catch sight of these shy and retiring creatures. Continue up the stony track to the right of Cockrigg Crags. Watch for the zigzags as height is gained. On reaching the upper limit of the plantation, go through a wall gap and head out across the open grassland on a faint path. Occasional cairns point you in the general westerly direction for High Tove, the grassy trail being quite easy to follow.

Be wary of an awkward rock step over the smaller tributary of Fisher Gill. A careless manoeuvre here could lead to broken bones. And when the wind begins to howl and moan with the intensity of a rabid banshee, beware the flitting shadows of long abandoned souls that are said to haunt these bleak heights above Armboth. Making their acquaintance could result in a permanent residency on the moor.

Precise footwork will eventually bring you to the welcoming dry island atop High Tove. A continuous fence stretches the entire length of the broad north/south ridge system. Head south, picking your way between stooks of heather across the marshy tract. Even in so-called dry seasons, drainage of this wild plateau is a none starter. Take heart from having double waxed your boots. (You did, didn't you?)

Beyond Middle Crag, the trail mounts Shivery Knott, a salutary oasis of rock amid the rolling heather. In another locale, this knoll would be of little consequence. Here, it assumes all the characteristics of a mini-Matterhorn. Could the person who named it have glimpsed the Armboth poltergeist?

Hurry down the far side and rejoin the fence. Follow it round past the prominent ridge of Bell Crags. On the right, set in a shallow depression, lies the inhospitable Blea Tarn. One of numerous in the Lake District, it is probably the least known.

Rounding the fence corner close to a rocky outcrop, the path drops down to cross a broad, level concourse. The fence heads due south, arrow-straight, towards the brutal uplift of Standing Crag. At the first gate, bear

left to descend a clear track following the infant valley of
Mosshouse Gill down to the
forest. A double gate in the
high retaining fence is meant to
prevent the escape of deer to
the open fell.

Under the oppressive can-
opy of vertical trunks, the path
continues its downward
course. It soon forks into a major forest road homing in from
the right which cuts a swathe
through the plantation, bearing north-east. After a short
time, the clear track passes
through a gate into one of the
few open wedges free of tree
cover. The path swings down
in two hairpin loops, beneath
the looming presence of Bank
Crags. At the far side beyond
another gate, continue down to
reach the valley road via a stile
100 metres to the south of
Hause Point.

A flight of stone steps leads
up to this prestigious viewing
site lunging out into the elongated fetch of the lake. Opposite, on the far shore, occurred
an incident that has led to the
place being called Clark's
Leap. Indicated on the old im-
perial OS maps but omitted
from current editions, the
rocky promontory appears to
have disintegrated.

The story is told of a jealous
husband who threatened to do
away with himself if his wife
continued her amorous flirta-

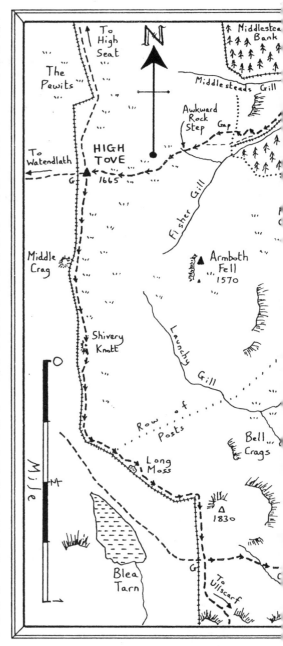

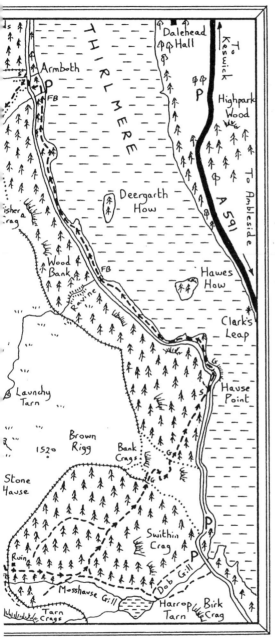

tions with local men. His entreaty ignored, the distraught Mr. Clark suggested hanging (no guarantee of success), then shooting (too messy and unpredictable). His wife felt that drowning offered the most agreeable form of termination. And so, at the appointed hour, they went to the lake, where the wife told Clark to take a mighty leap out into the gloomy pond to avoid the chance of injury on the rocks below. This he boldly did, and sank without trace. Satisfied that she had done her best to aid the plaintive fellow in his purpose, Mrs Clark strode away with nary a jot of conscience.

After returning to the road, go through a gate to take advantage of the lakeside path back to Armboth. A leisurely promenade in contrast to the busy line of communication on the far side, this tortuous trod winds between stands of mixed woodland skirting the lake. Breaches in the sylvan compass provide glimpses of Thirlmere's twin islands.

Rocky outcrops offer the chance to rest awhile and recapture a past that can only exist in the mind. All is now at peace on the western shore of the lake, except of course for one baleful day in the year when all hell is let loose. And we know when that is, don't we?

Walk 23

Mungrisdale: Immortality for Mungo

Mysteries:	St Kentigern GR 364305, Bowscale Tarn GR 336314
Distance:	6 miles
Total Height Climbed:	1450 feet (442 metres)
Nearest Centre:	Mungrisdale
Start and Finish:	Roadside parking is available alongside the River Glenderamackin in Mungrisdale. However, be prepared to fork out a £1 charge if you elect to park in front of the parish hall or on the fell access road adjacent to the telephone box. If you choose to begin at Bowscale, then copious free parking is available.
Map:	Ordnance Survey Pathfinder 576, Caldbeck

Secreted beneath the eastern wall that encompasses the fells at the back o' Skidda, Mungrisdale enjoys an enviable ecclesiastical heritage. For it was here that one of the most celebrated of early Christian missionaries left an enduring legacy that lives on today in the church dedicated to his divine passion.

Persecuted for his beliefs in Scotland, St Kentigern headed south to continue his religious teachings in Wales. On reaching Carlisle, he heard that settlers in Cumbria 'were given to idolatry and ignorant of divine law'. He decided on a detour into this wild mountainous territory and there established a central church based at Crosthwaite near Keswick.

His influence was such that eight churches remain today dedicated to the spiritual fervour of this single-minded cleric. All are located in the north of the region, which adds credence to the contention that this was where his conversion of the ungodly was concentrated. That situated in Mungrisdale has given the village its name, based on the priest's alternative Scottish title of Mungo where he became Bishop of Glasgow.

But it is Kentigern's mother who has provided us with the most intriguing story. Following a vow of chastity, she had spurned the advances of a neighbouring chieftain, much to the dismay of her father. He wanted the girl married off and banished her to toil as a servant in the fields. It was here that the rascally suitor happened upon the poor girl. His unwelcome attentions resulted in Thenew, as she was called, being left with child.

The punishment for such a shameful circumstance was death. Bound to a chariot wheel and driven down a precipitous hill, a miracle delivered her to safety amidst the shattered remnants of the vehicle. But justice demanded nothing short of the ultimate penalty and so Thenew was cast adrift in an open coracle. Washed ashore in the Firth of Forth, divine intervention once again stepped in to save the luckless maid.

In AD518 she gave birth to a sturdy boy who was raised to adulthood by a hermit. Christened Kentigern, he became Bishop of Glasgow by his twenty-fifth birthday. The young man embraced the Lord's work with gusto until he was forced to flee south after being persecuted for his beliefs. On reaching Carlisle, Kentigern was made aware of the need for deliverance of errant souls within the mountain fastness of Cumbria. At a time when the hearts and minds of the peasant farmers were taken by pagan worship, he faced an uphill struggle.

It is to his eternal credit that this pious individual managed to plant the first seeds of Christian endeavour within the region. Time should be left at the termination of this walk to visit the small church in Mungrisdale dedicated to the memory of St Kentigern.

The main path leading to the lonely fell country behind Mungrisdale

The Walk

But first, follow the rough track that takes advantage of the gap in the hills heading due west out of the village. Accompany the contrary flow of the River Glenderamackin, which here makes an abrupt swing around the shoulder of Souther Fell. Ahead on the right, Bullfell Beck issues from a deeply enclosed valley. Soon after the track swings to the left, cross the Glenderamackin using a short footbridge at a point where the two watercourses converge. The direct route continues upriver bound for Blencathra, but on a narrow path that is easily missed.

Much clearer is the obvious route which we take as it rises across the gnarled prow of The Tongue, a bulbous arm of Bowscale Fell comprising grey flakes of slate. Making a gradual ascent, the path enters the tributary

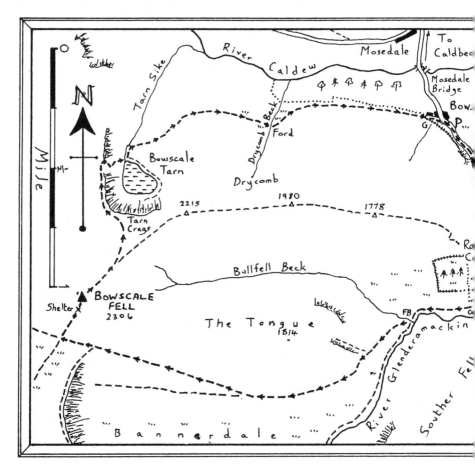

valley of Bannerdale, encircled by a forbidding necklace of splintered crags at its head. Watch for an indistinct right fork off the main valley track as you aim for the skyline.

Arrow-straight, the grassy groove is easy to follow and makes this the simplest ascent of any mountain over 2000 feet in the Lake District. And as you penetrate ever deeper into the heartland of the northern fells, sounds of human origin fade to nothingness to be replaced by a silence that positively resonates. It affirms one's belief that such areas of natural wilderness, untainted by the hand of man, must be treasured and preserved for future generations of fell wanderers to enjoy.

Keep to a westerly course once you have climbed above Bannerdale Crags, crossing a tract of marshy ground until a walkers' crossroads is reached. Take a right here up a shallow rise to gain the summit of Bowscale Fell. A half-moon shelter of rocks affords welcome protection from the rampant westerlies that bluster across these open tops.

On the day I arrived, threatening skeins of dusky cumulus hovered menacingly above the summit cairn. Before lunch had been consumed, the nebulous curtain had fallen. When leaving any remote locale in such circumstances, it is essential to be capable of translating map and compass skills into practice.

Immediately to the north-east of the shelter lies the true summit. Continue in the same direction for a quarter mile, when the decision has to be made as to whether a quick return to Mungrisdale down the broad shoulder of the east ridge is sought. The preferred route veers left. Pathless initially, it accompanies the upper rim of Tarn Crags in a northerly direction.

Soon, Bowscale Tarn emerges from the eddying gloom. Nestling in its ice-scoured hollow, remote from casual acquaintance, it is a gratifying vision after the suffocating mantle overhead. Descending further, watch for a thin path cutting down to the right which takes advantage of a chink in the tarn's armoured girdle. Initially quite steep, zigzags ease the descent, which is soon accomplished and brings you to the mouth of the corrie.

Backed by layers of chewed rock, the placid waters of Bowscale Tarn have been contained by a wedge of moraine deposited by the retreating glacier after the last Ice Age. Forged by the hand of some primeval sculptor, such a wild and romantic stage has produced the story of the immortal trout.

Wordsworth was sufficiently conversant with the myth to include it in his ode entitled *The Feast of Brougham*. Reference is made to the Shepherd Lord whose story is outlined in Walk 6:

> *His garb is humble; ne'er was seen*
> *Such garb with such a noble mien...*
> *The eagle, lord of land and sea,*
> *Stooped down to pay him fealty;*
> *And both the undying fish that swim*
> *Through Bowscale Tarn did wait on him;*
> *The pair were servants of his eye*
> *In their immortality;*
> *And dancing, gleaming, dark and bright,*
> *Moved to and fro, for his delight.*

Writing towards the end of the 18th century, the renowned historian William Hutchinson claimed that stars could be seen reflected in the dark waters of the tarn at midday. This particular phenomenon, however, has always been attributed to Blencathra's Scale Tarn, and it is strange that Hutchinson should have confused the two.

A clear track is joined at the mouth of the corrie, where Tarn Sike issues in torrid propinquity on its way to feed the insatiable thirst of the River Caldew. Wending a course eastwards, this was the fashionable route of early Victorians 'doing' the newly emergent Lake District tour.

On this side of Bowscale Fell, the impressive sweep of the Calder Valley is readily apparent. Secluded amidst the cluster of conifers below, pick out the Roundhouse that gives the isolated settlement its nomenclature. Down valley, the old farming hamlet of Bowscale stands at the entrance to this gap in the northern fell country at a distinct kink in the road.

Take a right along the road and continue for one mile, back to Mungrisdale, calling into St Kentigern's Church. Dating from 1756, the present building stands on the site of a much earlier one of 6th-century origin. Sit awhile in this tiny house of God admiring the individuality of the colourful, handmade hassocks.

Seek out a plaque to the memory of Raisley Calvert, a resident of Mungrisdale who suffered from consumption and was nursed by William Wordsworth before his death. Such was Calvert's gratitude that he left a bequest of £900 to the great man. After due deliberation, continue down the road to complete a walk of inestimable character, taking in a far-flung terrain that remains the preserve of the sagacious fell hound.

Walk 24

Seatoller: Along the Smuggler's Trail

Mystery:	Moses Rigg
Distance:	5½ miles, with Great Gable 6 miles
Total Height Climbed:	2000 feet (610 metres), with Great Gable 2400 feet (732 metres)
Nearest Centre:	Seatoller
Start and Finish:	This walk cuts out a substantial climb by commencing from the top of Honister Pass. An official car park is located behind the youth hostel.
Map:	Ordnance Survey English Lakes, 1:25 000, north-west area

In company with numerous other mountain situations, Honister Pass exhibits a distinctive dual personality. On the drive up from Buttermere, sombre turrets of fractured slate hang above the tortuous route in threatening mode. Riven from the scared torso of Honister Crag, mammoth chunks of rock lie scattered in wanton profusion across the narrowing valley head.

Truly an awesome spectacle not for the faint-hearted, it is little wonder that early tourists were apt to quake in fearful dread lest the debris loosened by the icy claw of Jack Frost should descend from the heights above. Such a cataclysmic display of nature's unremitting power was wont to leave the most hardened traveller mopping his fevered brow.

Open and much more light-hearted, the eastern approach from Seatoller provides a marked contrast. At the summit of the pass a slate works is still in operation, continuing a tradition established over centuries. Today it is motorised trucks that bring the raw material down from the quarries high on the moorland behind Fleetwith Pike rather than teams of hardy fell ponies.

The Walk

Our route begins by following the course of the old tramway that can be seen making a beeline for the western skyline. Avoid the main quarry road by initially taking a newly paved footpath section that has been laid to help contain severe erosion on this steepest section. Thereafter, the path continues ahead, following the original course, with wooden sleepers from the tramway still in evidence.

After passing through a noticeable rock cutting, the gradient eases and you soon arrive at a raised embankment. This marks all that is left of the drum house where the fully laden slate wagons were lowered down the tramway by a huge steel cable. From the pass, finished slate was then shipped down through Buttermere.

Before the 19th century, the main route contoured across the fells down to Wasdale and from there on to the port of Ravenglass. Known universally as Moses' Trod, it offers a first class approach to those bound for Great Gable. Sometimes referred to as Moses' Sledgate, it is unlikely that sledges were ever used on this rough terrain. More likely, this is a corruption of 'slategate'.

So who was the elusive pimpernel who gave his name to such a renowned trail? One of the will-o'-the-wisp characters who has added a splash of colour to local folklore, Moses Rigg is thought to have been a quarryman who decided to supplement his meagre earnings through the sale of illicit whiskey. Distilled from local bog water, the finished product was reckoned to be of the highest quality by customers of the rascally felon. So good, in fact, that when brought before the local magistrate the impounded cache was frequently returned. Doubtless the representatives of the law retained a supply for their own consumption, to be taken medicinally, of course.

Bear left at the drum house which marks the start of Moses' Trod. The path is clear underfoot. Initially across turfed moorland, it then climbs gradually around the western flank of Grey Knotts. An indistinct bifurcation soon forks right down into Ennerdale. Continue ahead on the main route to a line of old, iron fence posts.

Where the path veers to the left close to a prominent post, maintain a direct course ahead along a faint trail for 200 metres to rejoin the original line of the Trod. Thoughtfully engineered to avoid steep gradients, this route has not been commercially employed since 1860. Slate was thereafter sent down to the coast via Buttermere.

Rounding the grassy west shoulder of Brandreth, the savage bastion of Great Gable strikes the eye with the force of a rampant bull. No other mountain fastness imposes itself on the landscape with such dramatic grandeur. Gable Crag's mighty north face grabs the imagination as we make a slight descent to circumvent the headwaters of Tongue Gill.

But Moses Rigg would have had few qualms about making this trip, except perhaps from the unwelcome attentions of pursuing excisemen. Glancing back at regular intervals for the tell-tale signs of bobbing lanterns,

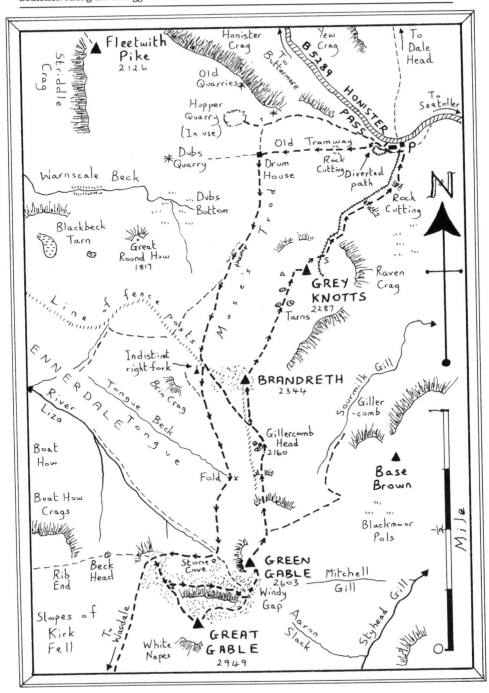

his pack train of whiskey-laden ponies would have maintained an easy pace into the remote amphitheatre of Stone Cove.

Huge boulders wrested from the fractured ramparts above lie scattered in wanton profusion below a tumbled splay of loose scree. A more poignant observation for Moses would have been whether his secret hide, located in a hut built high on Gable Crag, was safe from discovery. Now a ruin and difficult to access even for experienced scramblers, it would have made an ideal lookout post for the wily smuggler's confederates.

An obvious path can be picked out rising to the pass of Windy Gap, and may offer a quick means of gaining the ridge to Green Gable. **Do not be tempted!** It is rough and loose, and far less inspiring than the longer, though infinitely preferable Climber's Traverse. Looping round and across the upper reaches of the River Lisa in Stone Cove, climb the stony trail up to the north-west shoulder of Great Gable.

Moses' Trod continues down to Wasdale Head via Gavel Neese, where the smugglers would have enjoyed some welcome refreshment at the inn. Perhaps doing 'business' with the landlord at the same time.

Another valuable material probably smuggled by Moses would have been black lead or graphite. Mined near Seathwaite in Borrowdale and known locally as wadd, it was an extremely valuable commodity with a full pony load being worth £800. No mean sum even at today's rates, it led to much pilfering. Mine owners took drastic measures to contain the theft, but even regular strip searches failed to dent the resolve of the smugglers.

Our route takes a left up the rough, steep north-west ridge of Great Gable for about 200 metres. Watch for two strategically sited cairns that mark a gap at the start of the climbers' traverse. Here you must decide if the increasingly rough and stony ascent of Gable is worth the extra effort involved. Certainly if this is your first visit and conditions merit, I would utter the loud and clear epithet 'Go for it!'. Great Gable from this side has to be the toughest of all Lakeland mountain climbs. It is, indeed, a mighty challenge, reserved solely for those superhuman individuals with liquid hydrogen coursing through their veins who also consume three Weetabix for breakfast.

Mere mortals opting for discretion should follow the traverse which skirts the lower edge of Gable Crag. Pewter flakes of naked rock soaring above add fuel to the sceptics' claim that Moses Rigg could never have established a still in such an obscure locale. Decide for yourself while mounting a boulder-strewn chute up to Windy Gap.

This narrow col provides a stepping stone between the two Gables and is the easiest route onto Great Gable. Our way lies to the left up the short incline leading to the summit of Green Gable. A laudable mountain in its own right, most hikers use it merely as a staging post to the elder statesman across the deep cleft of Stone Cove. Are you the exception to the rule?

From the stony top, head north-east for a quarter mile then bear left down the rough northern shoulder to the depression at Gillercomb Head. Circle round a trio of tarns before slanting left across the flank of Brandreth. Upon reaching a line of iron fence posts, leave the cairned path to follow a direct course to the summit. Several of these posts have been commandeered by an inventive craftsman who has fashioned them into a bizarre sculpture adjacent to the more traditional summit adornment. Suggested names on a postcard only, please.

Continue in a direct line heading north-east across the intervening half mile to gain the craggy top of Grey Knotts. From this lofty eminence, head due east for 100 metres to locate a fence. Cross the stile and accompany this barrier all the way down the north face of Grey Knotts to Honister Pass. Beyond a distinctive rock cutting, the path has been newly paved.

Following in the footsteps of the legendary Moses Rigg provides a pleasant promenade through wild and romantic terrain. It allows a brief taste of the lifestyle, if not the produce of this mythical figure, who is the only person in the Lake District to have a highway named after him.

Unusual summit adornments on Brandreth looking to Great Gable

Walk 25

Pooley Bridge: Of Ghosts and Fairies

Mysteries:	Henhow GR 434177, the Sandwick Fairies GR 423198
Distance:	7½ miles
Total Height Climbed:	1900 feet (80 metres)
Nearest Centre:	Pooley Bridge
Start and Finish:	Ample parking space is available on the open grass area adjacent to the old church in Martindale.
Map:	Ordnance Survey English Lakes, 1:25 000, north-east area

More than any other Lakeland dales, those to the east of Ullswater require a substantial detour if they are to be visited. And once the hamlet of How-town is passed, a gear-crunching series of hairpin bends ensure that all but the most tenacious will be deterred from exploring the inner sanctum beyond. However, having breached the armoured citadel of brooding ramparts that guard secluded Martindale, the prospect of a veritable lost world opens up ahead. Split by the elongated ridge of Beda Fell, Boardale and Howe Grain provide walking of the highest quality, remote from the regular tourist honeypots.

Here is to be found a microcosm removed from contemporary stress and strain, where time has remained static. Silence reigns supreme amid the towering pinnacles that protect this idyllic corner of Eden. It is a place where age-old agrarian pursuits pay lip service to the 'missions' so beloved of modern commercial endeavour.

The Walk

From the old church in Martindale, cross Howegrain Beck on Christy Bridge to swing south up the valley. After passing Knicklethorns, the next building, a quarter mile further along the road, is a tumbled array of stones that once went by the name of Henhow. Now a ruined grey shell, there is nought here to indicate who once occupied the cottage. Broken walls, sad and forlorn, slowly crumble as the land reclaims its own.

Yet in this lonely outpost of rural Cumbria, a strange occurrence took place early one morning back in 1834. On leaving Henhow to tend his flock,

Ruins at Henhow have ghostly memories

a shepherd came upon a young woman following him on the far side of the road carrying a child. Somewhat disturbed at her sudden appearance as if from nowhere, the shaken man took heed as she began to relate a grievous story.

Forty years earlier, whilst living at Henhow, she had been courted and seduced by an unscrupulous local clergyman. Finding herself with child, the rascally poltroon made her consume a strong potion to terminate the pregnancy with the aim of protecting his reputation. Unfortunately, mother and child succumbed from the potent brew, their fate being to wander the roads in the district for one hundred years. It would appear that the scurvy cleric escaped retribution. Clearly a case of the devil protecting his own, for such a blackguard was surely no emissary of God. Let us hope that his comeuppance was duly administered in the next life.

The shepherd never fully recovered from his alarming experience knowing that the tragic spectre of a past resident still permeated his cottage. After 20 years, Henhow was abandoned never to be occupied again. It is now over a century since the sorrowful destiny of the poor woman came to an end, and she was finally allowed to rest in peace. But should you chance upon a young woman and child along the road, consider well this providential tale as you continue onward to Dale Head.

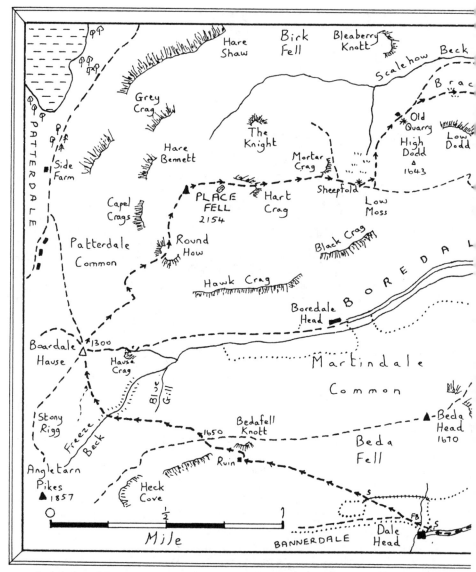

   This isolated farmstead lies at the end of the road at a point where the rising prow of The Nab cleaves Howe Grain asunder. Public access to the upper part of the valley is severely restricted as it has been turned into a sanctuary for the breeding of red deer. Herds of these reticent creatures can be observed by the watchful as you continue ahead up the bridleway. Im-

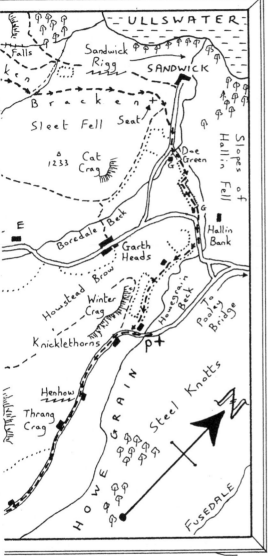

mediately before entering the environs of the farm, the right of way heads right over a fence stile and becomes the main access route linking Patterdale and Martindale. After crossing a small footbridge, accompany the wall on your left for 200 metres before forking right up the main track.

Pass through a fence stile to gain the open fell, carrying on up the steeply shelving eastern flank of Beda Fell. The well-graded diagonal ascent soon reaches a kink in the trail adjacent to an old shepherd's bothy below the outcrop of Bedafell Knott. A further 200 metres and the crest of the ridge is gained. Those of you suffering from the impediment of impatient spouses can return to Martindale along the narrow ridge over Beda Head.

Sparsely trod since the days when Patterdale was the nearest settlement for dale folk, this bridleway is a joy to follow as it circumvents the upper reaches of Boardale. Slanting down in easy stages, it crosses the clear-cut rift occupied by Freeze Beck then continues down to the major pass of Boardale Hause.

A broad, grassy saddle, this walkers' crossroads can appear confusing on close acquaintance in view of the array of paths veering off in all directions. Our way is clearly visible across the opposite side of the pass, shooting up the south ridge of Place Fell.

As height is gained beyond the main zigzag along the well-worn track, do not be tempted to assume the rocky knoll above to be the main summit.

This rough thumb of clawed rock is Round How, reached up a loose, stony channel. At the crest, the trig column atop Place Fell can be seen a quarter mile to the north-west across easy, rolling terrain. Mounted on a splendid plinth of bare rock, the summit makes a fine viewpoint across the vale of Ullswater towards the Hellvelyn ridge. A serene locale for reclining at one's ease as lunch is consumed.

Leave the rough top, heading north along a clearly defined path that makes a steady descent to the sheepfold at Low Moss. From this grassy depression, slant left into the valley of Scalehow Beck. The path then swings right through abandoned quarry workings. After a further 150 metres, our route forks right along a grass corridor in the bracken.

Maintain a right loop down the thickly clad bracken slopes, ignoring a track paralleling a tributary stream. Bear right down a half-concealed path to cross the watercourse, continuing around the lower flank of Sleet Fell. Take time to pause awhile on Peggie's Seat, a present given to a local lass on her 80th birthday back in 1990.

Below lies the secluded hamlet of Sandwick with the celebrated grassy dome of Sandwick Rigg overlooking Ullswater. Whilst taking stock of the varied craft plying back and forth along the placid reach, pay due regard to the legend of the Sandwick Fairies.

It was back in the 1850s, when Jack Wilson was returning home to Martindale over Sandwick Rigg that he descried a large group of fairies gambolling around on the grass in the moonlight. As he drew closer, a steep ladder could be seen reaching up to the nearest cloud. On seeing Jack rushing to join them, the little people scooted up the ladder and disappeared into fairyland, leaving a thoroughly perplexed fellow behind.

That was the last time fairies were seen in Lakeland, and Jack Wilson's final words regarding the sighting have evolved into a local saying, 'yance gane, ae gane, and nivver saw mair o' them.' Perhaps if more people were to believe in these impish creatures, they would return to add a bewitching charm to more of our walks. One can but live in hopes by exercising a trifle more imagination.

Angle down through the bracken to join the road for 100 metres before branching left along a side lane over Boardale Beck. Pass through a gate and follow this enclosed path round to the left then right up a rising slope to another gate. Regain the Boardale road along the access track serving an isolated house. Head left for 50 metres only before forking right along a walled path.

Pass right of The Lodge and then under the craggy bastion of Winter Crag, overshadowing the farm of the same name. On merging with the Howe Grain road, head left and back to the open grass common near Martindale Church.

Walk 26

Shap: Drowned in Mardale

Mysteries:	Dixon's Leap GR 443109, Mardale Green GR 475119
Distance:	6 miles
Total Height Climbed:	2100 feet (640 metres)
Nearest Centre:	Bampton Grange
Start and Finish:	The car park at the head of Mardale.
Map:	Ordnance Survey English Lakes, 1:25 000, north-east area

No finer dale head can be experienced anywhere else in Lakeland than that surrounding the feeder streams of Haweswater. Even with Manchester's source of corporation pop on full tap, nothing can overcome the sense of grandeur and majesty as one approaches the road end at Mardale Head. Truly, this is a land fashioned by giants with fell wanderers in mind.

For those who relish the feel of hard rock under their boots, this craggy fastness offers a veritable cornucopia to set the pulse racing and the heart pounding in anticipation. Laid out in perfect harmony, nature's treasure store provides a wild and romantic setting from which to engage in a walk of breathtaking intensity.

On the final approach to the head of the valley, on the right of the wooded promontory known as The Rigg, lies the site of Mardale Green. Drowned to accommodate an insatiable urban appetite for water, the village was dismantled in 1935 when the permanent residents of the graveyard were exhumed and reinterred in Shap cemetery. A further six years were to pass, however, before the area of water in the valley was effectively trebled and Mardale Green sank into the pages of history. Except during rare periods of drought when the ancient bones of the old settlement are resurrected, visits are now confined to those bound for the heights above.

Tracks forking off in all directions were once used by packhorses travelling between the valleys of Lakeland. Today, these hallowed portals have been infiltrated by modern day adventurers seeking to escape the pressures of a hectic society.

The Walk

Leave the road end to pass through a gate, making your way around the end of the lake and across a marshy section easily traversed using a series of walkways and bridges. Cross Mardale Beck on a footbridge and swing immediately left. Follow a stony track alongside the tumbling beck to a wall. Beyond the stile, the route slants right across rough ground towards another wall and the last manmade obstruction to be surmounted.

Entering the tributary valley of Blea Water Beck, the path keeps to the higher ground and avoids the worst of the marshy terrain. The path strengthens as the illusive corrie housing Blea Water is neared. A final short pull alongside the crackling flurry of the brew and there it is. Displayed to perfection, the classic proportions of this perfect armchair hollow are nothing short of awe-inspiring.

Generations of geography students have sketched this most wild and remote locale. Gouged out by the masterful tools of nature, Blea Water is Lakeland's finest piece of original architecture. Indeed, this is what the district is all about. Sit awhile and marvel in silent homage at the forces that have wrought such a creation while allowing the brooding air of mystery to wash over you. Such is the magnetic aura that has brought me back yet again.

Eventually it is time to leave, so make your way up the grass slope on the south side of the tarn towards the scarred rib ahead. Steep initially, with bare rock to contend with, this is a safe route if due care is exercised. Climbing above the circular tarn, you will soon realise that another jewel lies secreted in its own purpose-built corrie beyond Piot Crag. Small Water is the cousin of its more illustrious neighbour but no less impressive for that.

As the upper slopes ease, bear right to gain the gnarled and rather innocuous summit of Mardale Ill Bell. Barely higher than the surrounding plateau, there is nought here to detain us long so carry on around the rim of crags above Blea Water. Heading north-west, the path forks in to the summit wall that cuts a swathe across the top of High Street.

At the far side of the wall below the highest point, the original section of Roman road that gave the fell its name can still be picked out. Following the withdrawal of the Roman legions from Cumbria, this renowned highway continued as a cross-fell route for centuries. Known as Brettestrete or 'road of the Britons', it provided an important link between the west and east of the region. Later, it assumed the title of Racecourse Hill owing to the level nature of the upper concourse, which enabled the sport of kings to be conducted on local fell ponies. Convivial assemblages of shepherds gathering for the ritual exchange of stray sheep were followed by merrymaking on a grand scale. Identification of individual sheep was easily accomplished through the allocation of 'lug marks, wool strips and pops'.

In addition to racing, wrestlers grappled with each other whilst foot races were undertaken by those still able to stand. Long summer days ensured that the festivities often lasted for up to a week, or until the beer ran out. After 1835, the meet was moved down to Kirkstone Pass and thereafter to Troutbeck. Today, only buffetting westerlies scurry across the broad dome of the High Street.

Bawling in unrestrained fury through the cracks in the summit wall, one can sympathise with the marching legions that tramped across this bare fell side so very long ago. Listen carefully and you might just catch the faint commands of a weary centurion urging his men onward to Brocavum and a warm bed for the night.

From the trig column, make your way on a northeasterly bearing across the plateau to the rim of the ice-ravaged crags overlooking Blea Water, a thousand feet below. Here it was that in 1762 a certain fox-

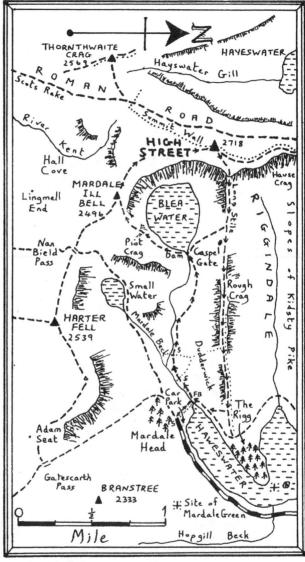

hunter named Dixon took a mighty tumble, falling hundreds of feet. Colliding with three rocky outcrops, the place became known as Dixon's Three Jumps. Suffering severe injuries, he still managed to point others following behind in the direction that the fox had taken before losing consciousness. He survived to pursue a less hazardous life in Kentmere.

The High Street ridge with Blea Tarn where Dixon fell whilst fox hunting

Avoid the fate of the feckless Dixon by locating the south ridge, which forms an arête between Blea Water corrie and Riggindale. Long Stile is a steep, rough descent but without difficulty. The views of upper Mardale whilst balancing along this superlative blade are second to none. Levelling out at the col of Caspel Gate, the path continues ahead to mount a rocky excrescence referred to appropriately as Rough Crag.

On the left lies the remote side valley of Riggindale, home to the only pair of nesting golden eagles in the Lake District. Constant watch is kept on the eyrie to ensure these noble birds are left in peace. Just beyond the gnarled apex on the Riggindale side but unseen from the ridge is located Hugh's Cave.

Hugh Holme escaped to the north of England after his plot to overthrow King John in 1209 was discovered. Hiding in the said cave, he stayed there until after the king's death. Having taken a fancy to Mardale, he remained to begin a dynasty known as The Kings of Mardale, which survived until the death of Hugh Parker Holme in 1885.

The path merges with a ridge wall and drops quite steeply once again towards The Rigg below. On reaching the enclosed copse of conifers, bear sharp right to return to Mardale Head alongside a wall. Retrace your steps to cross Mardale Beck and so return to the road end car park.

Walk 27

Penrith: Crossing the Fell of Fiends

Mystery:	Cross Fell GR 687343
Distance:	10½ miles
Total Height Climbed:	2350 feet (716 metres)
Nearest Centre:	Blencarn
Start and Finish:	Park on the main street of Blencarn. This parallels the road linking what have become known as the East Fellside villages, a string of small settlements on the eastern flank of the Eden Valley. Take the turn off signposted to Kirkland, which is easily missed.
Map:	Ordnance Survey Pathfinder 578, Appleby-in-Westmorland

Keep a weather eye on the western horizon as you walk down the village street of Blencarn to pass through the gate at the end. If a band of dark cloud hangs low above the Pennine tops, then beware the imminent stab from the Helm Wind. Centring on Cross Fell, this rampant blast cuts a ferocious sweep down through the gullies, howling in tormented agony like a thousand hounds from hell. Lying directly in its path, the chain of villages bear the remorseless brunt of its fury. Girding up around Brampton to the north, the Helm can last for three or four days leaving a trail of chaotic destruction in its wake.

Such awesome force has been known to have blown sheep around like scraps of paper, and once it was even rumoured that a horse and cart had been overturned, never to be seen again. So should a fearful baying of some tortured soul descend from the heights above as you set forth on this walk, take heed of nature's warning. You also may disappear into the clutches of this vehement barrage, unless you do as the locals and,

> '*When t'Helm low, and foxes bark,*
> *Bar up your door afore its dark.*'

Particular to this locality, due primarily to the contours of the escarpment fronting Cross Fell and its acolytes, it is little wonder that portents of evil characterise this apex of the Pennine Chain. On the day I last ventured up these fells, all was calm and serene, the 'Helm Cloud' a mere whisper dusting the undulating ridge top. Had the wind taken a belated vacation, or was it resting before once more gathering itself for the next virulent attack?

Wythwaite and some local residents in the shadow of Cross Fell

The Walk

Having determined to take a chance, slant left after passing through the gate to cross open, rough grazing. The path takes a north-easterly course past a large fishing tarn on the left. Soon after crossing Blencarn Beck, it enters a wide corridor, walled on either side and proceeding ahead between clutches of prickly gorse.

Stick with the wall on your right over Cringle Moor before crossing the depression adjacent to Wythwaite, the last habitation on this lonely trail. The elongated wall corridor narrows before terminating at a large sheep pen with a gate at each side. Beyond these, continue ahead towards Tottle Hill for 200 metres then swing right to cross Littledale Beck.

Clearly visible underfoot, the path now enters the constricting lower reaches of Littledale as it mounts the gently graded north slopes of Grumply Hill. Circling round to the right as height is gained, a grass shoulder above is home to rough-haired fell ponies. Our route surges ahead up the steepening incline then veers left across the broken face of Wildboar Scar, the first of a series of limestone stepped escarpments that characterise these west-facing slopes below Cross Fell. Above the Scar, the path leans right, mounting easy layered terraces.

Watch for a pair of distinctive cairns ahead and to the right. The path closes with these across stony ground, thereafter continuing in a north-easterly direction marked by a line of cairns. Beyond an isolated upright stone block, the route becomes somewhat indistinct underfoot as the approach to Crowdundle Head is made. And should a sullen band of grey swirl over the turreted scree wall, attended by a low moan of anguish, think well on these words from the pen of William Longstaff:

> *'Down Cross Fell's breast with maddening roar,*
> *The gusts commingle, rage and growl;*
> *Each grander, wilder than before.'*

Stick with the cairns when the path fades in tussocky grassland. It is resurrected at a higher level, eventually reaching the Pennine Way marker stone above the marshy col of peat hags. Here turn left up the stony incline which takes advantage of a breach in the defensive crag wall protecting the Cross Fell plateau. As the gradient eases, a stone monolith over 6ft (2 metres) in height hoves into view. Take a west-north-westerly course towards the next one on the horizon. Once past this, the summit trig column and shelter are soon reached across level ground.

Ranked as the highest point along the Pennine backbone, the fell was originally thought to be a conclave for aerial denizens and evil spirits. In consequence, it was accorded the name of Fiends' Fell by St Paulinus in AD644, and he 'celebrated mass and drove away the demons.'

Many travellers assert that they have been harried by these malevolent wraiths whilst crossing the fell. In hindsight, it would seem that the natural forces prevalent around the East Fellside are more than likely to have caused such trepidation. Yet anyone who chances to scan the wild moorland wilderness stretching away to all points of the compass cannot but empathise with such simple logic.

Once exorcised, a cross erected thereon was intended to keep these recalcitrant phantoms in their place. But it was not until the 17th century that the mountain became known as Cross Fell. Some have claimed it is short for 'Cross t' Fell' as early Christians who died in pagan areas were carried over the fell for burial at Alston.

Modern fell wanderers are provided with a rather decrepit cross-wall shelter in which to consume their butties. I well remember a previous visit when this was completely swathed in snow. Not a hint of the dreaded Helm Wind disturbed the cloying mist that transformed the summit into an Arctic whiteout. In these conditions, the ability to make use of map and compass assumed an urgency that was put to effective use.

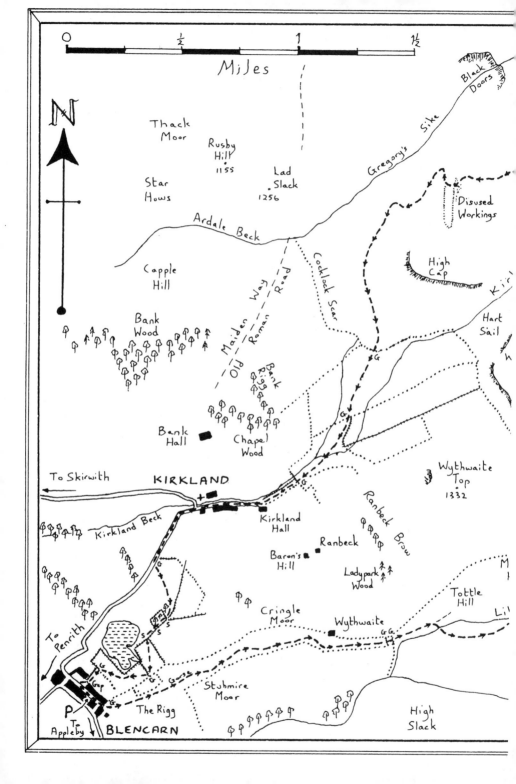

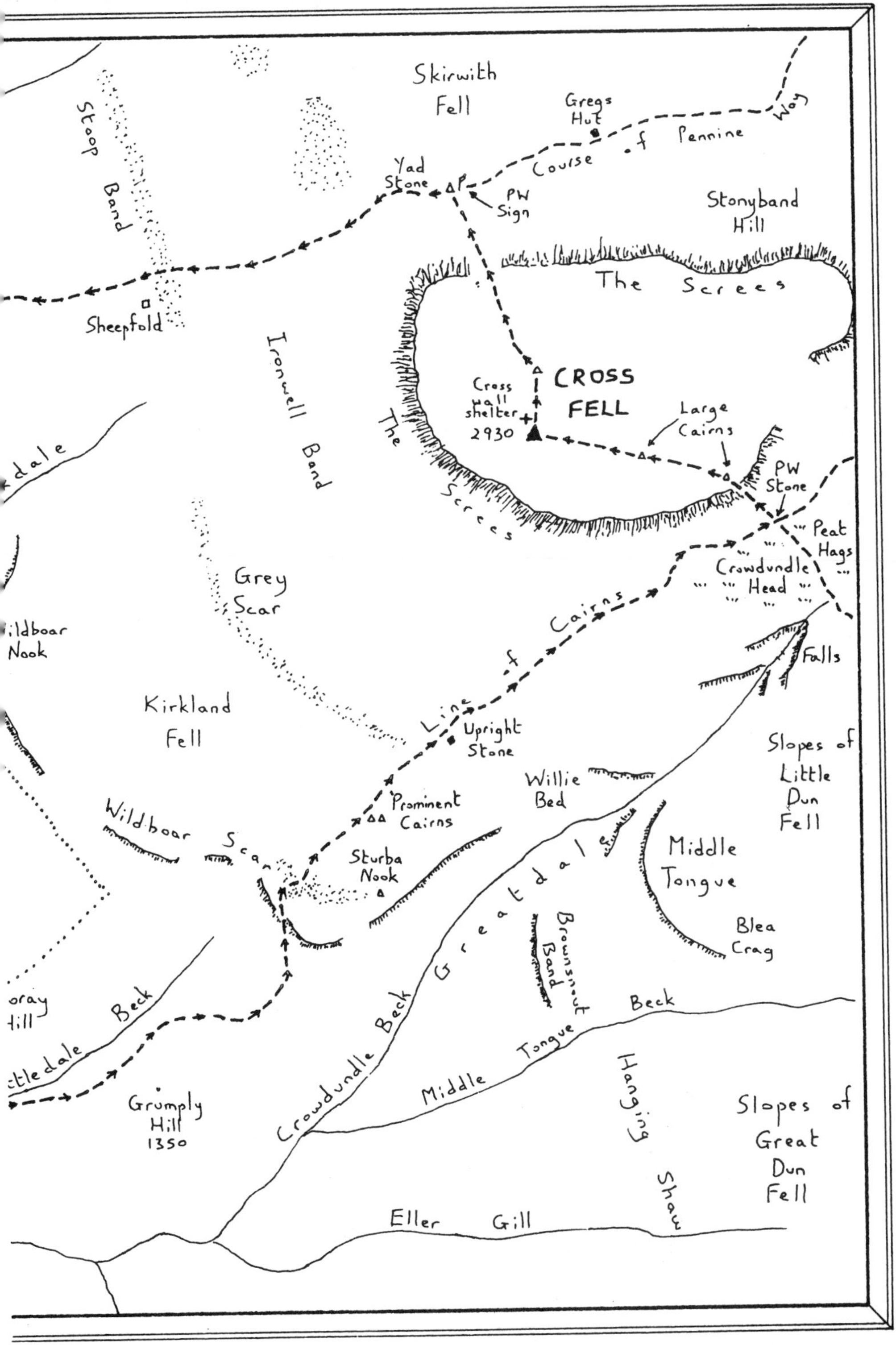

Skirwith Fell

Stoop Band

Gregs Hut

Course of Pennine Way

Yad Stone

PW Sign

Stonyband Hill

Sheepfold

The Screes

Ironwell Band

The Screes

Cross Hall shelter 2930

CROSS FELL

Large Cairns

PW Stone

Peat Hags

Grey Scar

Crowdundle Head

Falls

dale

Wildboar Nook

Kirkland Fell

Line of Cairns

Upright Stone

Willie Bed

Slopes of Little Dun Fell

Wildboar Scar

Prominent Cairns

Sturba Nook

Middle Tongue

Blea Crag

oray Hill

ttledale Beck

Crowdundle Beck

Greatdale

Brownsnutt Band

Beck

Grumply Hill 1350

Middle Tongue

Hanging Shaw

Slopes of Great Dun Fell

Eller Gill

Unfortunately, it is the giant golf ball perched on the tee of Great Dun Fell that commands the southern prospect. Reached by a road, this weather station has to be the highest occupied structure in the country, unless, of course, you know different. Turn your back on it by heading north from the shelter towards another prominent cairn 200 metres away and balanced on the rim of the plateau. Is it mere coincidence that this imposing edifice was built in the shape of a witch's hat, or is there a more sinister explanation?

Drop down towards the fractured ramparts that surround Cross Fell, aiming north-north-west for a further quarter mile down the fell side, towards the Yad Stone. Adjacent to this is a signpost marking the abrupt change of direction taken by the Pennine Way. Here we leave the celebrated long-distance highway as it bears right, continuing onward eventually to Kirk Yetholm over the Scottish border.

Our way flicks left along a clearly defined trail descending easy, grass-clad slopes. This route was once a corpse road connecting the village of Garrigill with the mother church at Kirkland. One such journey in the 17th century had to be abandoned whilst negotiating the hazardous trail in a raging blizzard. For two weeks the coffin was left close to the highest point until the snows abated and the delivery could be completed.

A simple stroll in fine weather for walkers, but not so for motor vehicles, even off-roaders. Encountering one such vehicle firmly entrenched in a hidden gully, the owner thanked me for the offer of assistance with assurances that he would soon be free. So I continued down Stoop Band.

On reaching the deep cutting of Gregory's Sike, take note of the craggy circlet of jagged teeth snarling at the valley head and known as Black Doors. Ahead, the track passes close to a side trough where miners once plied their arduous trade. Now long since abandoned, the workings have been largely reclaimed by the tough moorland sedges. Honeycombed by a maze of levels, much lead was extracted from the mountain before it became uneconomical.

A series of zigzags takes us down the final escarpment, the path slanting across the lower slopes below High Cap. Slipping gracefully through a gate in the intake wall, the track eases across the enclosed pastures through two more gates. Along a fenced section, the track runs alongside Kirkland Beck to terminate at the hall.

It had been my intention to inform the farmer that a vehicle was stuck on the moor, but suddenly the chug of a diesel engine heralded its arrival. A cheery wave from a mud-encrusted arm, and the 4x4 accelerated down the road, the owner no doubt chastened by his traumatic experience. One can never take the fells for granted.

Ambling down the single concourse of Kirkland, it is difficult to imagine that this diminutive settlement was once an important focus in the middle ages. Centred on the church of St Lawrence, soon passed on the right, it out-stripped all others in status.

Stride down the road to Blencarn, keeping an eye open for the signposted right of way 200 metres beyond the Skirwith turn on the left. Cross the field to the far left corner and enter a small wood over a fence stile. Exit at the far side in similar fashion to make your way along a fence close to the fishing lake. Step over a stile on the left to diagonally cross an adjoining field to its far corner, where there is a gate. Follow the fence on your right which slants away to the right after it rounds the next corner at the far side of the lake. Bear left to a fenced gate, where the course of the original path is rejoined.

At one time it made a bee-line straight across the lake, but as the ferry service has been discontinued, this detour was made necessary. A final walk along the fence and through a gap at the far end will bring you back to the main street of Blencarn.

Walk 28
Bassenthwaite: Through the Back Door

Mystery:	The Hermit GR 2427, Skiddaw House GR 287291
Distance:	10½ miles
Total Height Climbed:	2900 feet (884 metres)
Nearest Centre:	Bassenthwaite
Start and Finish:	A large parking area on the right, a quarter mile up the Orthwaite road off the A591.
Map:	Ordnance Survey English Lakes, 1:25 000, north-west area, **and** Pathfinder 576, Caldbeck

Although the lowest of Lakeland's summits of more than 3000ft, in my opinion Skiddaw is superior to the others. The roller-coaster ridge of broken slate is unmatched – it is an airy walkway falling away steeply on both flanks. Oceans of loose scree surround the high-level promenade, which affords an exhilarating stroll once the shifting layers have been breached. Normally ascended from the south, Skiddaw's distinctly moulded form has graced countless picture postcards dispatched to all points of the compass. Our route, however, approaches by way of a less-favoured though far more secluded backdoor.

Skiddaw Forest has long since abandoned any pretensions towards extensive tree cover. The sole arboreal presence within this central amphitheatre remains the windbreak behind Skiddaw House. Once a remote residence for local shepherds, it has since been refurbished as a youth hostel. Isolated and lonely, the bleak location of the stone dwelling only serves to accentuate the wild nature of this heather-clad bowl.

Comprising the oldest rocks not only in Lakeland but the whole of Europe, the brittle, flaky texture of Skiddaw Slate has led to the formation of smoothly angular fells. They provide a stark contrast to the jagged upsurge within the heartland of the District. And Picasso himself could not have planned the geometric phrasing more accurately. The mighty Skiddaw would assuredly merit the highest accolade in Cubist design.

Beside the shepherds, one other person is known to have taken up residence upon the mountain's austere fastness. George Smith of Banffshire occupied a cave in 1864, before the bare slopes were given over to the current blanket of coniferous woodland. A learned man, George earned a living painting portraits of the locals and was well versed in religious matters, having once considered entering the priesthood. On occasion he would venture into Keswick, where a penchant for hard liquor would be assuaged in the numerous hostelries. The inability to ration his intake often resulted in vehement outbursts and a night's lodging in a police cell. Forced to leave the district by those who constantly hounded the lone hermit on account of his eccentric ways, George Smith eventually died a pauper in his native Scotland. His ghost is said to wander the lower slopes of Skiddaw searching for those who drove him away.

Approaching Skiddaw from the west

The Walk

Cross the stile immediately beyond the car park and take a clear path over a stream, aiming for the line of trees ahead. Keep left of these, continuing ahead up a grass bank to a wall gate and then across the next field to a wall stile. Beyond this, with a wall on your left, approach Barkbeth, crossing a fence stile and then bearing left down a broad corridor to the deep cut valley of Barkbeth Gill.

After another stile, the path swings to the left above the valley, aiming north towards Hole House. Here, a descending zigzag crosses the beck on a bridge that has made the original ford redundant. Stride out over the field aiming north-east, initially through a gate and then a stile before another gate brings you to the easy fording of Mill Beck.

Immediately after, cross a stile and accompany the clear track around a fenced field to mount the facing lower slopes of Cockup. Keep the fence on your left, passing through two gates before it changes to a wall. At 1250 feet (380 metres), we pass through the final gate of the intake wall and on to the open grass fell.

Bear left around the smooth northern slope of Cockup, keeping close to the wall. As the valley of Dash Beck is entered, stick with the higher path that contours into the deep ravine of Dead Beck. Emerging, the path maintains the same height, eventually making a gradual descent to merge with the main upcoming track. Join this as it climbs above the tumbling cataract of Whitewater Dash. Above your right shoulder the lowering presence of Dead Crags pervades the atmosphere, hanging above the trail like the sword of Damocles – so a sigh of relief as the route climbs above the falls to cross the beck into the upper valley.

Cutting an arrow-straight vector through the tangled heather, the access road to Skiddaw House enables rapid progress to be made into this wild and lonesome tract. Vast and silent, hemmed in by the rolling fells, this is fine walking territory to be savoured at one's leisure.

After a slight descent to cross the headwaters of the River Caldew, climb the facing slope to reach Skiddaw House. Nowhere else in Lakeland houses such an austere tenement, dedicated to shepherds who once spent their lives removed from civilisation in this remote outpost. For forty-seven years the resident shepherd was Pearson Dalton. He lived at Skiddaw

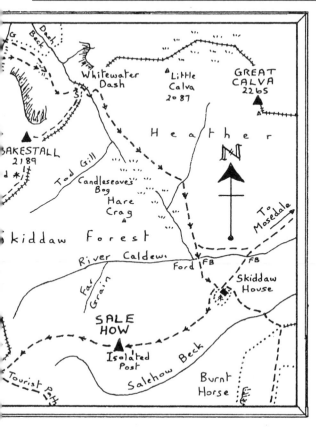

House all alone during the week but maintained a link with civilisation by staying with his sister at Fellside, south of Caldbeck, on weekends. With a battery powered radio and a few tattered books for company, Pearson enjoyed his hermit-like existence and saw no reason to retire. Sometimes cut off for weeks on end due to blizzards and snow drifts, age eventually caught up with the old recluse and he was compulsorily retired in 1969.

Having paid due homage to past traditions, and acknowledged that life today is a doddle in comparison, bear right alongside the surrounding wall. Continue up the eastern flank of Sale How on a clear path through the grass, noting a distinctive wooden post that probes the skyline ahead. This is not the summit, which is higher up and more to the right. The neat cairn is a recent addition which attempts to provide Sale How with a degree of pre-eminence it certainly deserves in this locality. All around is grass on this side of the valley, in contrast to the dense mantle of heather cloaking Great Calva to the north-east.

Circle round the shallow saddle to climb the facing incline in a wide left-hand loop towards the depression separating Skiddaw from Little Man. After falling in line with the upper fence, the tourist track from Keswick is soon gained. It is appropriately still a bridleway – early tourist climbers rented horses to make the ascent!

Perhaps the most famous was made in 1794 by the novelist Mrs Radcliffe. For a woman this was, indeed, a bold and reckless escapade. On reaching the apex, she claimed the air had become 'very thin' and the path 'scarcely wide enough for a single horse'. Exaggeration maybe, but the intrepid lady was at least prepared to venture into territory which most people at the time held in morbid dread.

Pony treks continued to be the principal means of attaining the summit until the First World War, when the tariff was six shillings (30p) with extra for the guide. A local guide book of the day offers sturdy horses 'for those who are unequal to the fatigue of ascending the mountains'. Such reminiscences hark back to an age of gentility, when the mountain stronghold was still held in fearful awe by the majority.

How things have changed. Make a right through the iron gate and follow the clearly defined concourse on to the south top and thence along the exposed rim to High Man – the main summit. In addition to the trig column and shelter, a plaque permitting identification of distant landmarks now adorns the noble edifice. On state occasions in the past a great fire was lit on the top of Skiddaw, which was clearly visible from Carlisle.

One such fire was lit by Robert Southey and the Wordsworths to celebrate the Battle of Waterloo in 1815. William accidentally upset the boiling kettle needed to dilute the punch, which meant that neat rum was drunk by all. Merry indeed must have been the descent from the summit by boisterous revellers barely able to cling to their jolting mounts.

Return to the shallow depression immediately prior to the south top and fork right down a path that becomes increasingly steep and loose as height is lost. Aiming south-west towards Carlside Col, the route is clear but needs great care if painful abrasions to one's tender parts are to be avoided.

From the broad col, bear right down the scree-choked entrance to Southerndale. Initially pathless, an old track emerges in the grass to the right of the beck, lower down, beyond a sheepfold. It follows the valley sides, avoiding the floor which becomes marshy in mid-course.

When the intake wall is reached, the track fords Southerdale Beck, entering the lower pastures by a stile. Swing round to the left through another stile, heading due west for 200 metres when yet another is negotiated. Continue ahead for 100 metres before the grass path veers sharply to the right to chaperone a line of thorn trees. At the T-junction, bear left to retrace your steps back to the car park.

This walk is the premier means of experiencing the true measure of Skiddaw's unique appeal. Easy of ascent for a 3000-footer, it was a favourite with Victorian gentlefolk and remains popular today. Approaching through the backdoor avoids all unnecessary contact with others of the human race should this be desired, except of course during the latter stages.

On days when the mist hovers like some heavy, dank shroud and the cold wind moans through the rough tussocks, spare a thought for the ethereal presence of George Smith and sympathise with his eternal plight.

Walk 29

Buttermere: Beauty and Buttermere

Mystery:	Mary Robinson of the Fish Hotel GR 174169
Distance:	7 miles
Total Height Climbed:	700 feet (823 metres)
Nearest Centre:	Buttermere
Start and Finish:	Approaching Buttermere from Newlands Hause, make use of the roadside parking available on the right close to the road's junction with the B5289.
Map:	Ordnance Survey English Lakes, 1:25 000, north-west area

Surely there can be no more perfect setting for a village than that enjoyed by Buttermere. Sited midway along this classic example of a glacial trough sporting not one but two ambrosial lakes, rugged ice-carved peaks jostle for position on either flank. Hemmed in by such an illustrious entourage has led to the valley being described as enclosed and secretive, one in which the visitor feels something of a trespasser.

Many of the early tourists regarded Buttermere as another Eden, even though it was one of the least accessible spots. Or perhaps it was because of the considerable effort involved in negotiating the passes which brought them here that they really appreciated its appeal.

Many visitors came to gaze upon the celebrated Beauty of Buttermere, whose bewitching charm and grace had so eloquently been reported by the eminent 18th-century travel writer, Joseph Budworth. Captivating the hearts and minds of those who met her, Mary Robinson lived with her family at the Fish Hotel where she waited upon the guests. Even Wordsworth was entranced by the young girl's demeanour and unquestioned virtue, reminding his friend Coleridge some years later that they were both 'stricken by her modest mien'.

But fate was soon to deal the innocent belle a dastardly hand in the form of the Honourable Augustus Hope MP. Hearing of this divine creature whilst staying in Keswick, the devious conniver set off for Buttermere and proceeded to woo her with charismatic persuasion. Married in 1802, the marriage was ill-conceived from the start and proved to be short-lived. Not trusting the fellow on account of his rough vulgarity, Coleridge delved into his past and found him to be an impostor and a fraud. His true character was soon revealed to all in the London edition of the 'Sun', barely a month after the wedding.

An accomplished trickster, John Hatfield, a humble commercial traveller, was found to have tricked his way into the hearts and pockets of numerous other gullible females prior to his courtship of Mary Robinson. Not only that, but he was, in fact, already married with a child whom he had abandoned in Somerset. Realising that the game was up, Hatfield fled the district, but was soon arrested and brought to trial at Carlisle assizes. Found guilty of bigamy and the more serious charge of forgery, he received the ultimate penalty and was hanged on September 3rd, 1803.

National publicity of the case turned Mary into a celebrity. Continuing to work at her father's hostelry in Buttermere, she handled the notoriety with decorum and patience, eventually marrying a Caldbeck farmer and living happily ever after. An appropriate finale for a young woman whose tragic tale was dramatised for all the country to gloat over.

Home of the clebrated 'Beauty of Buttermere'

The Walk

Ponder over this remarkable happening whilst ambling down the road past the church and village hall to turn left at the Bridge Hotel. Pass the Fish Hotel on the right, where Mary Robinson lived and worked, to take the rough, fenced lane through a gate bearing south towards Buttermere lake. Ahead, the fine ridge stretching from High Crag to Red Pike captures the eye, no less impressive now than it was back in Wordsworth's day.

Take due note of the slanting scree shelf below the looming bulk of High Crag and known locally as Sheepbone Rake. A successful ascent of this rent in an otherwise insurmountable circle of crags will raise the humble fell wanderer to the dizzy realms of a true mountain personage.

Pause for a moment on the flat valley pasture to marvel at the tremendous U-shaped profile. To the south-east, the mighty prow of Fleetwith Pike remains stranded above the waterline like an ancient galley after cleaving the dale head in two. Only nature, exhibiting her artistic traits for all to see, could have fashioned such an idyllic tapestry.

Beyond a second gate, stick with the fence and then go over a footbridge straddling Buttermere Dubs to gain the lakeside path through another gate. This stream connects the two lakes of Buttermere and Crummock Water, which have been known to merge on occasion after periods of heavy rain.

Turn left alongside Buttermere, avoiding the obvious track striking up through the woods. This is the popular route direct to Red Pike. Instead, follow the lakeside path which soon splits. Adopt the upper course, climbing gradually through the coniferous enclave of Burtness Wood. Watch for a grassy sward forking right located 100 metres beyond the gap in a broken wall. This meanders through the plantation to the upper edge of the wood, where a fence stile gives access to the open fell.

A thin, stony path picks its way across the steep cant, keeping above the forest wall. At the end of Burtness Wood it veers in to meet the wall which then mounts the steep slope into the higher level of the intake fields at the entrance to Burtness Comb. Leave the wall at this point to strike uphill on the right of Comb Beck into the heart of the corrie proper.

The main path aims for the north-east ridge of High Stile. Our route bears left towards the splay of towering ramparts ahead, our objective being the rake soaring up on the left of Sheepbone Buttress. The inspiring grandeur of this bold façade might well reduce lesser mortals to the consistency of a quivering jelly. Not so you, dear reader. Trust in GKD and you will not be led astray. Steep and rugged it may be, but, nevertheless, quite straight forward.

Cross Comb Beck and begin the ascent of the lower boulder field. Beware of loose stones secreted amidst the thick mantle of vegetation. A thin track emerges as height is gained, becoming more pronounced on the right side of the Rake, which makes for an easier ascent. When the upper limit of the Rake is reached above Sheepbone Buttress, bear right to scramble up the steep though easy north face on to the broad summit ridge of High Crag.

This sensational climb will hopefully stir the blood and inspire the heart, creating a ravenous appetite for more of the same. Above Comb Crags, the ridge heading north-west gives intimate yet safe glimpses into the climber's world of Burtness Comb from aloft.

Rusted iron posts extend the entire length of the ridge beyond Red Pike and are a useful guide in mist. The ridge path makes a parabolic swing to the subsidiary summit of High Stile, which is actually a metre higher than the main top a quarter mile to the west. From this rocky eminence, cross the upper ledge above Chapel Crags, keeping right of the main path to enjoy a bracing descent on a rock stairway. Then, continue around Bleaberry Comb to make a gradual ascent to the clear-cut pyramid of Red Pike. The eastern delineation affords a solid idea of its distinctive shading, achieved through the presence of syenite in the soil.

Where Sourmilk Gill enters Buttermere, a distinctly reddish tinge can be observed upon the placid waters. One story to account for this concerns a

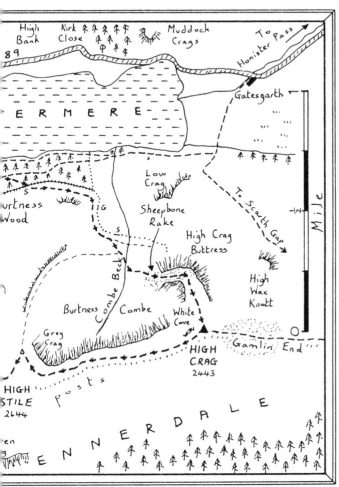

raid on Borrowdale by the Scottish Clan Graeme. Beaten out of the valley over Honister Pass by the defenders, a young chieftain slain upon the battlefield was laid to rest in the crags above the pass. His life blood is said to have flowed down into Gatescarthdale Beck and so into the lake, causing the mysterious stain.

Descent from this splendid dais begins on a well-worn path heading due east before making a sharp left down an exceptionally loose flank bound for Bleaberry Tarn. Fork left away from the main path to reach The Saddle, a low col between the rampant force that is Red Pike and its trusty watchdog known as Dodd.

From the col, head north-west down a clear trail into Ling Comb, keeping a lookout for an abrupt zigzag which descends through the dense, heathery pile to a cross-fell wall. Pass through a gap and bear left, down towards Far Ruddy Beck. On reaching a small cairn, leave the obvious route which continues ahead to strike right, down a thin trail into the deciduous woodland clothing the lower valley slopes.

As height is lost the path fades and the gradient steepens appreciably, with Far Ruddy plunging down in a series of mighty cataracts hidden amongst the trees. Pick your way down to join the valley track near the southern end of Crummock Water, close to a sheepfold. Bear right for a half mile before crossing Buttermere Dubs at Scale Bridge and then proceeding along a fenced track back to the village. If time permits, slake your thirst at the bar of the Fish Hotel, named after the char which inhabits Buttermere.

Here it was that Mary Robinson played hostess to ardent admirers two centuries before. Today, it is her namesake towering over the small village and the accompanying retinue of elegant courtiers that visitors come to feast their eyes upon.

Walk 30

Braithwaite: The Bishop's Challenge

Mystery:	The Bishop of Barf GR 218264
Distance:	5 miles
Total Height Climbed:	1650 feet (503 metres)
Nearest Centre:	Thornthwaite
Start and Finish:	Park in the recessed area opposite the Swan Hotel at Powter How, one mile north of Thornthwaite.
Map:	Ordnance Survey English Lakes, 1:25 000, north-west area

And finally, the ultimate challenge that has accorded this walk the status of being last in the book. This is not merely to gain the summit of Barf, an easy enough task if the Beckstones Gill route is selected. No, this is a frontal assault that all fell walkers worthy of the name must embrace at some point in their booted careers.

Culminating in the precipitous downfall overlooking Bassenthwaite Lake, Barf forms the crusty shoulder of the loftier though rather prosaic dome of Lord's Seat. As such it provides the only breach in an otherwise continuous blanket of coniferous green ranging along the lake's western flank. Serried ranks of fir, pine and larch have conquered the lower slopes with ease. So far, the upper, grass-clad sward has resisted this onward march, and, I hope, will always retain an indomitable resilience.

On the approach to Thornthwaite, a white extrusion soon catches the eye on the lower slopes of Barf's rough torso. This is the celebrated Bishop of Barf. Boldly adorned in vestments of purest white, this ecclesiastical patriarch preaches from a somewhat precariously sited pulpit. Doubtless the bulk of his sermonising was aimed at carousing topers who were seen to prop up the bar of the Swan Hotel below.

Rumour has it that a certain inebriated punter once laid a bet that he could ride his horse to the very top of Barf. Reaching only as far as the point where the Bishop now resides, he tumbled down the shifting scree to finish in a tangled heap in the vicinity of the Clerk's domain. Once you have attempted to gain a foothold on the noble dignitary's perch, it will rapidly become clear that this is a legend having its origins at the bottom of a quaffed tankard or three.

The Walk

Make your way along the path at the rear of the parking area to merge with the back lane to Beckstones. Watch for a fence stile on the right, after which a firm path leads up to the Clerk. Cloaked in white, this fang of rock points the way up a crumbling escalator. This ascent should not be undertaken lightly due to the brittle nature of Skiddaw slate.

Barf's stirring ascent is reserved solely for those who aspire to feats of gladiatorial combat. Mere mortals will attempt this frontal assault at their peril. If discretion is your middle name, continue ahead along the valley trail to cross Beckstones Gill 100 metres higher up. Beyond a stile, follow the trail through the dense phalanx of conifer plantings. After climbing above Birch Crag, the path eventually reaches the upper limit of the plantation, where a stile gives access to the open fell. Cross the easy, rolling terrain to gain the summit with no loss of dignity, nor damage to one's anatomy.

Mean machines in the mould of Warrior and Rhino will accept the challenge with gritted teeth, psyching themselves up for the coming fray. Make use of the subsidiary map for the ascent, the first objective being the Bishop's roost, entailing a steep haul up the initial ocean of fragile scree. Only stalwart leviathans wil continue beyond.

Eventually arriving at the glistening, white-washed rock, consider this whimsical yarn related by an old farmer. The Bishop in question was said to have a vicious tongue, and frequently castigated his flock with ill-deserved abuse. Accusations of infidelity, sloth and greed were hurled about with impunity, having no regard for the distress

A precarious pulpit for the Bishop of Barf

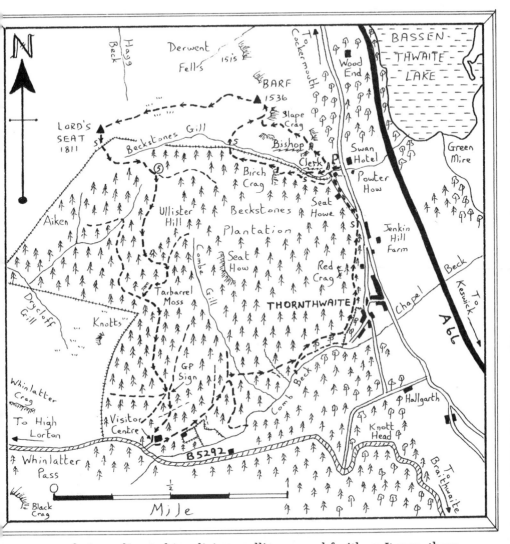

caused. Appealing to his religious calling proved fruitless. It was, therefore, decided to consult with a higher authority in order to control these un-
warranted attacks. And so the Bishop of Barf was finally silenced.
Entombed within a block of stone where all could bear witness to the
shameful besmirching of his cloth, he shall remain thus whilst the Clerk remains on guard below.

Having joined the disgraced priest on his airy dais, the way ahead is clear

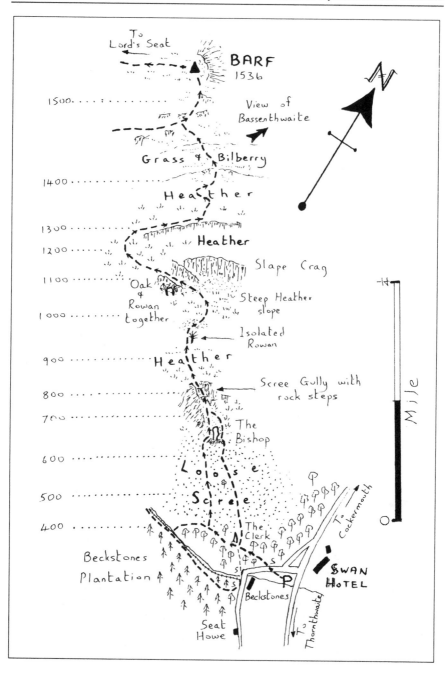

but no less arduous. Special care must be exercised in view of the steep gradient and fickle movement of the loose trail underfoot. Keep right initially, where the heathery outcrops allow a degree of security, before slanting left up the stony chute above. A series of precarious rock steps must be negotiated to gain firm ground.

Climb up through the heather to a lone rowan tree, after which the path levels out for a few metres. Veering to the right up a steep cant, the thin path picks a way through steep heather towards the striking bastion of Slape Crag. Progress beyond this savage buttress is achieved by making a left towards the base of the crag.

Take advantage of an exposed track, passing above an oak and rowan to cross more heather-clad slopes on a thin trod. Once the main crag has been by-passed, strike up to round the left edge of a higher escarpment. Circle to the right along the lip of the crag line until the path slants left uphill. Cloaked in grass and bilberrry couches, these upper slopes are infinitely easier, and the main track from Beckstones Gill is soon joined above. Lean to the right for a simple stroll across open ground to the summit of Barf.

Most impressive of the views from this lofty site has to be the profile of Skiddaw and its satellites across the yawning gulf occupied by Bassenthwaite. And you are now in a position to appreciate that any challenge made to ride a horse up the front of the mountain would indeed have been the height of folly.

Leave the summit heading due west on a clear track around the upper reaches of Beckstones Gill. Lord's Seat rises above the rim of the forest less than a mile distant. Cross open, rough pasture, marshy in places, to gain the crown, located 100 metres west of the fence erected to contain the burgeoning tree growth.

The throne from which the fell has acquired its name lies 10 metres to the north-west. A rocky hollow of baronial proportions, it proffers a regal setting from which to admire the majestic vista towards Criffel whilst partaking of an equally peerless lunch.

From here, drop down to the edge of Beckstones Plantation and cross the fence stile. The path, laid with fence poles for ease of passage, meanders across the bare upper slopes, soon curving left past a scattering of conifers. Watch for an obvious right junction opposite yellow-capped marker post number five.

Accompany this trail along the upper edge of the forest and around the western side of Ullister Hill. Entering the main tract of forest, the route snakes round a clear trail passing a line of bare crags on the right. Soon after, a major forest road T-junction is reached at Tarbarrel Moss.

Bear left along the wide road that drops down between dense stands of conifers to a key route focus identified by the Grisdale Pike forestry sign.

After noting the amendments being made to the regimented line of previous tree plantings, take the partly-concealed path on the left of the sign. This descends through the trees until a nature trail is reached. Head right down a steepening gradient, past an adventure playground to arrive at the Whinlatter Forestry Commission Visitor Centre.

Thornthwaite Forest merits the distinction of being the first of its kind that was planted by the newly created Forestry Commission with the express aim of restoring timber supplies after the First World War. Over 200 varieties of tree have been planted here, to improve the amenity value of the area as well as for commercial usage.

Ever sensitive to public scrutiny, the Commission are quick to indicate the positive aspects of forestry. Nature trails and orienteering courses have been designed to encourage public awareness of the need for woodland and its conservation. Forest Enterprise is proud to have established what is believed to be the first orienteering course in the world catering to the diverse needs of the disabled.

Well worth a browse, the centre provides a wide range of entertaining alternatives to encourage care of the forest environment. Having been suitably stimulated, walk east from the centre past a lone bungalow down a forest road. Ignore the first track slanting left and continue to a sharp, right-hand hairpin bend.

Continue ahead along a narrowing trail for another 50 metres until a path branches right into the sepulchral confines of the tree cover. Descending at an easy pace, the path crosses a tributary stream feeding into Comb Beck. It then parallels the beck before merging with another major forest road. Do not cross straight over but take the road heading left, which rises slightly before swinging left above the village of Thornthwaite.

Stick with this wide trail until it terminates on the back lane serving Beckstones Farm. Head left up the lane past Seat How for the return to the car park. This walk establishes a vivid contrast between the brash exposure of the Barf Challenge and the closeted isolation of the silent forest, which complements the mysterious aura surrounding the Bishop and his acolyte.

NORTH LAKELAND
WALKS with CHILDREN

Mary Welsh
with illustrations by Christine Isherwood

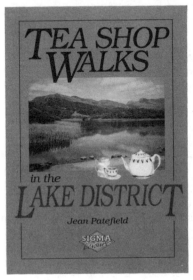

TEA SHOP WALKS

in the

LAKE DISTRICT

Jean Patefield

100 LAKE DISTRICT HILL WALKS
Gordon Brown
£7.95

LAKELAND WALKING: on the level
Norman Buckley
£6.95

MORE **LAKELAND WALKING: on the level**
Norman Buckley
£6.95

MOSTLY DOWNHILL: Leisurely Walks in the Lake District
Alan Pears
£6.95

LAKELAND ROCKY RAMBLES: Geology beneath your feet
Bryan Lynas
£9.95

PUB WALKS IN THE LAKE DISTRICT
Neil Coates
£6.95

TOWN & VILLAGE DISCOVERY TRAILS: Cumbria & The Lake District
Norman Buckley
£6.95

IN SEARCH OF SWALLOWS & AMAZONS: Arthur Ransome's Lakeland
Roger Wardale
£7.95